2 to 22 DAYS IN NEW ENGLAND

THE ITINERARY PLANNER

1991 Edition

ANNE E. WRIGHT

John Muir Publications
Santa Fe, New Mexico

Originally published as *22 Days in New England*

For Randy, without whom this book would not have been possible.

Special thanks to my parents, Linda and Alex, for their research assistance and to Richard Harris for his support and guidance throughout the project.

John Muir Publications, P.O. Box 613, Santa Fe, NM 87504

1991 Edition

Library of Congress Cataloging-in-Publication Data
Wright, Anne E., 1959-
    2 to 22 days in New England : the itinerary planner / Anne
E. Wright. — 1991 ed.
      p. cm.
    Updated ed. of: 22 days in New England. 1st ed. c1989.
    Includes index.
    ISBN 0-945465-88-2
    1. New England—Description and travel—1981- —Tours.
I. Wright, Anne E., 1959- 22 days in New England. II. Title.
III. Title: Two to twenty-two days in New England.
F2.3.W75 1991
917.404'43—dc20
                                      91-7324
                                       CIP

Design/Production Mary Shapiro
Maps Randy Johnson
Cover Map Jim Wood
Typography Copygraphics, Inc., Santa Fe, New Mexico
Printer McNaughton & Gunn, Inc.

Distributed to the book trade by
W. W. Norton & Company, Inc.
New York, New York

CONTENTS

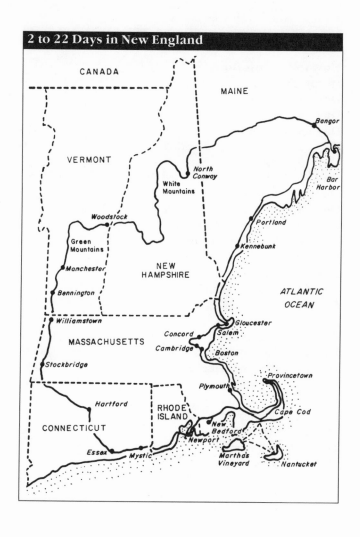

2 to 22 Days in New England

CANADA

MAINE

VERMONT

Bangor

North Conway

White Mountains

Bar Harbor

Woodstock

Portland

Green Mountains

Kennebunk

Manchester

NEW HAMPSHIRE

ATLANTIC OCEAN

Bennington

Williamstown

Concord

Gloucester

MASSACHUSETTS

Salem

Cambridge

Boston

Stockbridge

Plymouth

Provincetown

Hartford

RHODE ISLAND

Cape Cod

CONNECTICUT

New Bedford

Newport

Essex

Mystic

Martha's Vineyard

Nantucket

HOW TO USE THIS BOOK

Your New England tour begins in Boston, Massachusetts, one of the nation's oldest cities, and ends there three weeks later after a 1,200-mile loop through some of the nation's most scenic and historically significant terrain you'll find anywhere. Although this may not seem like a lot of ground to cover during the course of your vacation, believe me, your 2 to 22 days will be chockfull of engaging activities, adventures, and picturesque sights.

New England is the birthplace of our nation in many respects. The pilgrims landed here in 1620, the first battle of the Revolutionary War was fought on Massachusetts soil, Harvard University in Cambridge is the cornerstone of American education, and founding fathers such as John Adams spent their lives here. You'll feel history all around you as you pause on centuries-old town greens, drive past crusty stone walls that define property lines, ramble over covered bridges, and visit time-weathered historic homes and monuments. Along the way, you'll see where Shakers worshiped, poets penned, colonists rebelled, whalers toiled, and presidents were born.

Nature has endowed New England with a beautiful landscape. Atlantic currents and ice age glaciers have sculpted this part of the country to near-perfection. During your holiday you'll have the opportunity to stretch out on sparkling white sand beaches, picnic in rocky coves, watch playful seals in their natural habitat, hike pine-covered trails, stand atop the highest peak in the Northeast, swim in bubbling mountain streams, and dine on fish recently snatched from the ocean while breathing in the salty sea air. If you're lucky, you'll also see the hills ablaze with vibrant colors as winter approaches.

This guide opens the door to your New England adventure. It has been organized for quick reference in an itinerary format divided into 22 daily sections containing:

1. A **suggested schedule** for each day's travel and sightseeing.

2. A detailed **travel route** description for each driving segment of your trip.

3. **Sightseeing highlights** (rated in order of importance: ▲▲▲ Don't miss; ▲▲ Try hard to see; and ▲ See if you get the chance).

4. **Lodging, campground,** and **restaurant** suggestions for each night of the trip.

5. **Helpful Hints**—random tidbits that will help your trip run smoothly.

6. **Itinerary Options**—excursion suggestions for travelers who have extra time.

7. User friendly **maps** designed to show you what the road up ahead is really like.

Why 2 to 22 Days?

For those who have about three weeks of vacation this year, "2 to 22 Days" itinerary guidebooks can help you use that time to the fullest extent by directing you to the best a region has to offer. How often have you wasted precious time off just trying to locate a decent restaurant or missed out on a treasured museum because you spent too much time in a disappointing one? In *2 to 22 Days in New England*, I've done the legwork for you so that your holiday will be as trouble-free and enjoyable as possible.

The itinerary, my ideal trip, includes a sampling of sights everyone should experience on a visit to New England, personal favorite haunts, and a realistic time frame in which to see them all. The daily schedules will help you structure your days but are not carved in stone. Use them flexibly to create the best trip for you. For instance, if art history is not your thing, skip the Boston Museum of Fine Arts on Day 2 and go to the Computer Museum instead, or spend the afternoon gorging on Fenway Franks at a Red Sox game.

What if you have less than 22 days? No problem. One of the nicest things about *2 to 22 Days in New England* is its adaptability. The itinerary is created for those who have three weeks, but if you only have one, pick the week that interests you the most.

The route begins and ends in Boston because it is the easiest point of entry for those traveling to New England from afar; however, the itinerary can be joined anywhere. Given the compactness of New England, no stop on the itinerary is more than a 3 ½ -hour drive from Boston, with the exception of Bar Harbor, which is about 6 hours. Those living in or near Boston can certainly use two- and three-day segments of the trip for a number of weekend getaways.

When to Go

This itinerary is designed for travel between mid-May and mid-September. Many historical sites, restaurants, and hotels listed are only open during those months when the climate is at its best. Of course, New England is known worldwide for its spectacular fall foliage, which generally reaches its peak in Vermont and New Hampshire in early October. Winter skiing is also a popular attraction there. Do keep in mind that if you visit New England for the foliage or for skiing, many of the suggested sightseeing highlights will already be closed for the season.

July and August are the busiest months in terms of tourists, and the most expensive—particularly in the coastal regions. Vermont and New Hampshire are naturally very crowded during peak leaf-peeping season, when places like North Conway in the Mt. Washington valley of New Hampshire turn into veritable parking lots on Columbus Day weekend. If you plan to travel during peak periods, advance lodging reservations are a necessity. I've been told that churches have had to open their doors to stranded tourists, or worse, weary travelers have spent frosty New England nights upright in their cars. For your trip to run as smoothly as possible, I recommend calling ahead for reservations.

Personally, I think September is the best time to see New England. The weather is usually sunny and pleasant without the heat and humidity of July and August, ocean temperatures are at their warmest, and many sites are still operating on their extended summer schedules. You may miss the foliage at its peak (although I'll bet you'll see a few leaves turning in the northern regions), but you'll also miss many of the summer tourists, and off-season rates begin just after Labor Day in some coastal towns.

June is another good time to travel and avoid the crowds, but the weather is less predictable than in September, and high-season rates generally go into effect on Memorial Day weekend.

Transportation
Just about all of the principal airlines have several daily nonstop flights to Boston from most major U.S. airports. Prices vary depending upon your departure city, but fares from airline to airline are generally comparable. Your travel agent can help get you the lowest-price flight available for your desired departure date. It is usually best to purchase your ticket at least 30 days in advance to secure the lowest fare.

While the metropolitan Boston area is readily accessible by public transportation and a network of commuter trains and buses, the rest of the trip is not. Greyhound, Bonanza, Peter Pan, and Vermont Transit bus companies serve the more rural areas of the itinerary to some extent, but you will find it hard to travel to all the sights once you reach each destination by bus.

This trip is designed for those traveling by car, RV, or motorcycle. With the exception of Sargent Drive along Somme Sound in Maine, all suggested routes are open to those types of vehicles. However, the auto roads to Cadillac Summit in Acadia National Park and to Mt. Washington in New Hampshire may be too precarious for larger motor homes.

For aesthetic reasons, this suggested route follows secondary highways rather than major interstates in most cases. This means your average driving speed will be 45 to 50 miles per hour rather than 55 or 65. Distances between New England destinations are relatively short when compared to other parts of the country, so speed

and travel time are not major factors in trip planning.
You'll be able to appreciate the surrounding countryside
better at slower speeds. You'll also find that states such as
Maine, New Hampshire, and Vermont are very good
about marking historical sites, lodging, and eating establishments that are off these secondary roads with directional and mileage signs.

Renting a Vehicle
All major car rental agencies have offices in Boston. Compact cars rent for about $200 per week with 700 to 1,000
free miles weekly. Subcompacts are somewhat cheaper
and get better gas mileage but can feel cramped when
you spend a lot of time inside them.

Traveling by rental recreational vehicle is another possible way to explore New England. A 20-foot RV sleeping
up to five people rents for about $680 weekly during
June, $940 during July and August, and $415 during the
winter months. These base rates don't include add-on
charges for collision insurance, vehicle preparation, pro-
pane, and the like. In the Boston area, RVs can be rented
from West Suburban Leasing at 70 Prospect Street in
Somerville. Call them at (617) 437-7500 for rental information, or contact their parent company, Cruise America,
toll-free at (1-800) 327-7778. Keep in mind that while
touring by RV is a convenient way to travel, renting one
will only mean significant lodging savings if you are
traveling with more than two people.

Lodging
Country inns are one of the best ways to truly immerse
yourself in New England tradition. Inns, some of which
have been operating for 100 years or more, serve regional
specialties, are often furnished with priceless antiques,
and generally offer comfortable to exceptional lodging,
sometimes at little more than the cost of a motel room. A
night in a country inn averages about $90 for two during
the summer and about $60 off-season. In many cases, the
room rate includes a full breakfast, making the cost more

appealing. Motels in the area average about $55 for two but often provide only half as much in the way of amenities and atmosphere. However, if you're traveling with a family, motels may be the only affordable lodging other than camping. For those who really want to travel lavishly, I have also listed luxury accommodations.

Camping is a much cheaper alternative to staying in either bed and breakfasts or motels, although many campgrounds on the itinerary are not as convenient to the sights. Campgrounds operated by state, national, and municipal park services usually charge less than private campgrounds—about $8 to $12 per night. Park-run campgrounds tend to be more wooded and less crowded than private ones but often don't have facilities such as hot showers, grocery stores, playgrounds, or swimming pools on the premises as many private camping areas do. Of course there is a price to pay for convenience: nightly rates at private campgrounds run from $14 to $18—or more. To get the most satisfaction from your trip, choose the type of lodging that best suits your life-style and budget.

Food
Preparing your own meals is the most economical way to eat on your trip, and you shouldn't have any trouble finding adequate provisions at any point along the way. If you're not equipped for food preparation or prefer to leave that task to others while on vacation, be prepared to spend an average of at least $3 to $5 for breakfast, $5 for lunch, and $10 for dinner, per person, when eating out. The restaurants I suggest are ones that I've personally enjoyed, or that have local reputations for their food quality, uniqueness, convenience, or price. Fresh seafood is what comes to mind first when one thinks of New England cuisine, but places like Boston and Cambridge offer the visitor a wide variety in ethnic dining as well.

An ice chest or a disposable styrofoam cooler, stocked with soda, juice, yogurt, cheese, and other snacks, can save both money and time. If your bed and breakfast sends you off with a hearty morning meal, you can often get by until dinner with just a yogurt in the early afternoon. If your lodging establishment doesn't provide breakfast, a chilled fruit cup from the cooler may be just the thing to start the day. By cutting out one restaurant meal a day, you can reduce the total trip cost by more than $100 per person. Having the cooler will also save time since you won't have to pull off the highway every time you feel a pang of hunger or thirst. Besides, the less time you spend dining, the more time you'll have to explore the New England you came to see.

Licenses
Since campfire and fishing regulations vary from state to state, it is wise to check with each state prior to engaging in either activity. Most states require fishing licenses (Maine sells theirs at the Tourist Information Center in Kittery), and in some areas permits are required for campfires.

What to Bring
Mark Twain once said, "One of the brightest gems in the New England weather is the dazzling uncertainty of it." There couldn't be a truer statement, so the best way to deal with New England weather is to come prepared. Even in the hottest summer months, it is possible to run into cool evenings in parts of Maine, Vermont, and New Hampshire. Bring at least one heavy sweater no matter what season you plan to visit the area. The sweater will also come in handy any time you are out on the Atlantic, whether it's on a whale-watching vessel, the ferry to Nantucket, or a small pleasure craft; the ocean breezes can be quite chilling.

Although hopefully you won't have occasion to use it, raingear is a must when traveling through New England. It is unlikely that you'll be able to spend three weeks there without encountering some form of precipitation, even if it is only a soft island mist on Martha's Vineyard. I recommend packing a lightweight hooded poncho to use while cycling or hiking and a fold-up umbrella for city sightseeing.

Binoculars will help bring the scenic vistas and wildlife of Acadia and the White Mountains National Forest into closer view, so make room in your suitcase for a pair. You wouldn't want to miss seeing the seals basking on the rocks just off the Maine coast.

Also pack a small empty knapsack or daypack. It should be large enough to hold your sweater, poncho, guidebook, map, camera, and binoculars but lightweight enough to carry easily on your back. You'll find it invaluable when hiking, traveling to the islands, or simply transporting a picnic lunch.

Recommended Reading

Reading (or rereading) *The House of Seven Gables* by Nathaniel Hawthorne, *Little Women* by Louisa May Alcott, *Ethan Frome* by Edith Wharton, and *Walden* by Henry David Thoreau will complement your New England sojourn as you visit the haunts and homes that inspired these great American literary classics. The many layers of Newport, Rhode Island, society were the basis for Thornton Wilder's enjoyable *Theophilus North*, while Henry Beston spent a Thoreau-like year in a tiny house on Nauset Beach in Cape Cod recording the passage of nature in his book *The Outermost House*; either book will add an extra dimension to your trip. Robert McCloskey's *Make Way for Ducklings*, a delightful tale of a duck family living in the Boston Public Gardens, will help the city come alive for young children.

As a supplemental guidebook, *The Complete Guide to Bed & Breakfasts, Inns & Guesthouses in the United States and Canada* by Pamela Lanier (Santa Fe, N.M.: John Muir Publications, 1991) will help you locate that perfect country inn. FODOR'S New England guide is a good background information source for those who wish to stray from the 22-day itinerary.

ITINERARY

DAY 1 Arrive in Boston and get settled in your hotel. Then put on your walking shoes. Today you'll visit the USS *Constitution*, Old North Church, Paul Revere's House, and the Bunker Hill Monument—all stops on Boston's renowned Freedom Trail. Round out the day browsing through Quincy Market's smart shops, sampling delicacies from the Market's main food hall, strolling along the nearby waterfront, and dining in one of the area's restaurants.

DAY 2 Today you'll explore Boston's museums: Isabella Stewart Gardner's Venetian Palazzo and the Museum of Fine Arts are two of the city's most beautiful. At sunset, get a bird's-eye view of the city from the Hancock observation deck, and have a late dinner along posh Newbury Street.

DAY 3 Cross the Charles River to Boston's sister city, Cambridge, and bustling Harvard Square. Harvard University's outstanding museums await art, history, and science devotees, or you may prefer to saunter through the college's ivied courtyards or amble past Brattle Street's stately homes, including that of poet Henry Wadsworth Longfellow.

DAY 4 Travel to historic Concord to stand on the site of the first battle of the Revolutionary War. Take in colonial period rooms at the Concord Museum or visit the home of writer Louisa May Alcott. Picnic at Thoreau's Walden Pond; then it's on to Lexington for the Museum of Our National Heritage.

DAY 5 There is more to hunt than witches in the beguiling city of Salem, and today you will unearth some of the city's hidden treasures.

DAY 6 Driving along Massachusetts' "other cape," Cape Ann, you'll see the eccentric Hammond Castle and the fishing port of Gloucester, lunch by the sea in the artist colony of Rockport, and then continue up the coast to Kennebunk, Maine.

DAY 7 Today you'll travel a large portion of Maine's celebrated coastline, passing through the picturesque villages of Camden, Rockport, and Wiscasset, to reach Bar Harbor by evening.

DAY 8 Glorious vistas atop Cadillac Mountain and the pounding Atlantic surf await you today in Acadia National Park, the easternmost U.S. national park.

DAY 9 Give Acadia and Bar Harbor a last lingering look before you proceed across central Maine. After you pass through Gorham Notch, the scenic panorama of New Hampshire's Presidential Range from Mt. Washington's summit is the high point of the day. Late afternoon is for unwinding in Jackson, or poking through shops and factory outlets in nearby North Conway.

DAY 10 Beautiful scenery abounds as you continue through the White Mountain National Forest. You'll see Crawford and Franconia notches and the Old Man of the Mountain and perhaps hike the Flume Trail. Stop for the night in charming Woodstock, Vermont.

DAY 11 Enjoy Vermont's Green Mountains, picturesque villages, maple syrup, and delicious cheddar cheese.

DAY 12 Spend the day in the college towns of Bennington and Williamstown, viewing folk art by Grandma Moses in the morning and French impressionist works, among others, in the afternoon.

DAY 13 The spartan life of the Shakers at Hancock Shaker Village makes an interesting contrast to the more traditional American life-style depicted in colorful oils at the Norman Rockwell Museum in Stockbridge. Today you will observe both. A classical concert at Tanglewood or modern dance performance at Jacob's Pillow caps off a memorable day in the Berkshires.

DAY 14 Travel southeast from Stockbridge into Connecticut and follow the Connecticut River valley, making stops in Hartford, the state's capital, and the river towns of East Haddam and Essex. The night will be spent in the coastal town of Mystic.

DAY 15 Take a trip back through maritime history with a visit to the nation's largest maritime museum, Mystic Seaport. Then let yourself be entertained by thousands of aquatic creatures at Mystic's Marinelife Aquarium.

DAY 16 To get a glimpse of the greener grass on the other side of the fence, tour Rosecliff or the palatial Breakers, two examples of the lavish summer "cottages" built at the turn of the century by wealthy families such as the Vanderbilts. After the mansions, get a fresh breath of salty sea air along the Cliff Walk, or stroll Newport's downtown wharf area where boutiques and boats entice the visitor.

DAY 17 Depart for Cape Cod, stopping along the way in the whaling port of New Bedford. Visit Heritage Plantation and Sandwich Glass Museum in Sandwich, Cape Cod's oldest town.

DAYS 18 and 19 Spend these two days bicycling, beach-combing, and window-shopping on the islands of Nantucket and Martha's Vineyard.

DAY 20 Return to Cape Cod and travel its length to artsy Provincetown. Explore the spectacular sand dunes of the National Seashore along the way.

DAY 21 You'll travel from spirited Provincetown, along Cape Cod's scenic Route 6A, to historic Plymouth, the site of the Pilgrims' first settlement.

DAY 22 Return to Boston to end your three-week journey where it began, stopping in South Shore seaside villages and at the John F. Kennedy Memorial Library along the way.

BOSTON

Your New England tour begins in New England's largest city, and one of the nation's oldest—Boston, Massachusetts.

Suggested Schedule

9:30 a.m.	Visit the Public Gardens.
10:00 a.m.	Begin your all-day tour of Boston's Freedom Trail.
1:00 p.m.	Lunch in the Italian North End.
2:00 p.m.	Cross over to Charlestown on the Freedom Trail to visit the USS *Constitution* and Bunker Hill Monument.
5:30 p.m.	End your day browsing in Quincy Market's smart shops, then dining in one of the area's restaurants.

Arriving in Boston

Although Logan Airport is only 2 ½ miles from downtown Boston, getting to the downtown area can often be an exhausting experience. If you're renting a car, *don't* pick it up at the airport. Wait until Day 4 when you are ready to leave the city and begin your trip up the coast. Cab fare into the city will run at least $10, and can be very expensive if you get stuck in traffic, which you're bound to do. But a taxi may be your only option if you have a lot of luggage. Share a cab if possible. (Some downtown hotels will pick up guests from the airport, so you may want to call and check with your lodging to see if they offer such a service before jumping into a taxi.)

If you are traveling light, the MBTA (Massachusetts Bay Transportation Authority) is the fastest and least expensive means to reach the downtown area. A free shuttle bus that stops regularly at all airline terminals will take you to the Blue Line subway stop. A subway token is $.75, and in ten minutes you'll be in the heart of Boston. Board the train on the "Inbound" side of the tracks. A map of the entire subway system is clearly posted in every subway station to help guide you to your destination.

Another option when traveling to downtown is to take the Water Taxi from Logan Airport. This is a quick and scenic method, but unless your hotel is located on the waterfront, you'll still have to transfer to some other mode of transportation once across the harbor.

Amtrak trains arrive at South Station several times a day from New York and points south. South Station is on the main subway line, and no doubt your hotel will only be a short subway or cab ride away.

Greyhound operates a terminal in the city, providing access to Boston from many smaller towns. The depot is near the Arlington Street subway stop of the Green Line in Back Bay.

By car, Boston can be reached from the west by the Massachusetts Turnpike, from the north by Interstate 95 to Route 1, and from the northwest and south by Interstate 93 (the southern portion just below Boston is locally known as the Southeast Expressway).

Getting Around

Walking is the preferable form of transportation in this compact city. Be sure to wear comfortable shoes, since many of the old brick and cobblestone streets were in place long before high heels came into vogue.

The subway system is the oldest in the country and sometimes operates like an antique. The network of lines (Red, Green, Blue, and Orange) is quite extensive in the heart of the city, but check your street map before hopping on the system. Often three stops on the subway are only three physical blocks apart, and it would take more time to wait for the train than to walk the distance yourself. The farther one travels from the city center, the more it makes sense to travel by subway, but it is best to avoid subway travel at rush hour. Tokens are $.75 each, and in some areas, additional fare is required. Subway stations are marked by a "T" symbol.

Since Boston has been settled for over 350 years, a great number of existing thoroughfares were laid down over old cowpaths that follow no logical pattern. The haphazard network of streets can be confusing to out-oftowners, and parking spaces are hard to come by. Don't try to demystify Boston driving, or tame Boston drivers, in three short days. Boston is meant to be enjoyed on foot.

Boston

Boston was established in 1630, and you get a sense of its long history the moment you arrive. It is hard to walk more than a block in downtown Boston without seeing some kind of historic marker. If it weren't for the parked cars, a walk at dusk along Beacon Hill's gas-lit brick side-walks and cobblestone streets might convince you that you'd traveled back in time to the nineteenth century.

With the exception of Back Bay, a former tidal marsh area that was filled in and laid out in the mid-nineteenth century, Boston's complex network of narrow streets, dis-tinct neighborhoods, and old brick buildings give it more the feel of a European city than of a modern American metropolis.

However, one only need look at the number of glass skyscrapers in the financial district to realize that progress has by no means passed Boston by. In addition to the thriving financial community, countless high tech firms have moved into the area during the last 15 years. Boston Harbor, once the city's mainstay, is still a busy port. Long a center of learning, Boston boasts one of the greatest concentrations of higher education institutions in the nation and is on the cutting edge of medical research. Consequently, it is an interesting, culturally diverse, and attractive city, steeped in its past yet vibrantly alive in its present.

Sightseeing Highlights

▲▲**The Boston Public Gardens**—Founded in 1897 and designed by Frederick Law Olmstead, who also created New York's Central Park, these are the oldest pub-lic gardens in the United States. The gardens are in full bloom from April through October, but the stately trees and beautiful landscaping make them a pleasure to visit in any season. Children will love the "Make Way for Duck-lings" sculpture, depicting a scene from the book of the

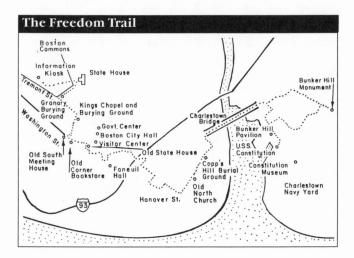

The Freedom Trail

same name, and a ride on Boston's own Swan Boats. A swan boat ride is a relaxing way for adults to get perspective on the city as well. The boats operate from 10:00 a.m. to 4:00 p.m. mid-April through mid-June and 10:00 a.m. to 5:00 p.m. mid-June through Labor Day (weather permitting). A small fee is charged.

▲▲▲**The Freedom Trail**—The trail is a 3-mile walking tour of many of Boston's historical sites. It begins at the information booth in Boston Common on Tremont Street between the Park Street and Tremont Street subway stations. Sightseeing tours also travel the 3-mile route. You can get tour information from the visitor information kiosk. Though the trail is well marked by a red line on the pavement, it is a good idea to get a trail map at the information booth in case you decide to stray from the main route. The map also contains background information on each site.

The first stop on the Freedom Trail is the "new" **State House**, designed by respected architect Charles Bullfinch and built in 1795. The Capitol was built on land belonging to John Hancock's family, and Samuel Adams laid the cornerstone. The State House can be toured free from 10:00 a.m. to 4:00 p.m. Monday through Friday.

The next stop is the **Park Street Church** and **Granary Burying Ground** where John Hancock and Samuel Adams lie buried near victims of the Boston Massacre. A little farther down Tremont Street is **King's Chapel,** built in 1754. Behind the chapel on School Street is the **Old City Hall,** now home to a marvelous French restaurant, Maison Robert, and a commemorative statue of Benjamin Franklin. Several doors down on the corner of School and Washington streets is the **Old Corner Bookstore** in a lovely brick building that dates back to 1712. Now known for its fine selection of regional and travel titles, the store is steeped in literary history: such notable literary figures as Henry David Thoreau, Henry Wadsworth Longfellow, Ralph Waldo Emerson, and Judge Oliver Wendell Holmes met there in the 1800s to discuss topics of the day.

Diagonally across from the Old Corner Bookstore at the **Old South Meeting House,** you can view a multimedia presentation on the building's role in history: Boston Tea Party rallies were held here. The meeting house was built in 1729. Admission is $1.75 for adults, $1.25 for seniors and students, $.50 for children 6 to 18. Hours are 9:30 a.m. to 5:00 p.m. daily April through October, and 10:00 a.m. to 4:00 p.m. weekdays and 10:00 a.m. to 5:00 p.m. weekends during the rest of the year.

The Old State House at Washington and State streets is the next stop on the trail. It was built in 1712 and currently houses exhibits on Boston history. Admission to the museum is $1.75 for adults, $1.25 for seniors and students, $.50 for children 6 and up. It is open daily from 9:30 a.m. to 5:00 p.m. Just outside the State House is the site of the Boston Massacre, where five colonists were slain by British soldiers in 1770, foreshadowing the Revolutionary War.

From the State House you'll pass through **Faneuil Hall** and **Quincy Market,** old buildings that have recently been refurbished to serve as a major focal point for entertainment, dining, and shopping in the city. Return this evening for a more leisurely visit.

From Quincy Market, cross under Interstate 93 to
Boston's thriving Italian North End. Visit Paul Revere's
home before treating yourself to a memorable lunch in
one of the North End's fabulous bistros. The **Revere
House**, built in 1676, is the oldest building still standing
in the city of Boston. Admission to the house is $2 for
adults, $1.50 for seniors and students, $.75 for children 5
to 17. The house is open daily from 9:30 a.m. to 5:15 p.m.
during the summer, from 9:30 a.m. to 4:15 p.m. during
the winter, closed on Monday during January, February,
and March. **The Pierce/Hicborn House** next door can
be toured with the Revere House for a combined admission charge of $3.25 for adults, $2.25 for students and
seniors, $1 for children.

After lunch, pick up the Freedom Trail again and visit
the **Old North Church** where the famed lanterns ("one
if by land, two if by sea") warned of the British arrival the
night of Paul Revere's ride. Farther up Hull Street, you'll
pass the old **Cop's Hill Burial Ground** where Edward
Hartt, the builder of the USS *Constitution*, was buried.
Cross the Charlestown Bridge to the Charlestown Navy
Yard to view his creation, also known as "Old Ironsides."
The ship was built in 1797, saw active duty in the War of
1812, and is the oldest commissioned warship afloat
today. There is also a USS *Constitution* museum, open
year-round. Admission is charged for the museum, but
the ship itself is free. Museum hours are 9:00 a.m. to
6:00 p.m. in the summer, 9:00 a.m. to 4:00 p.m. in the
winter, 9:00 a.m. to 5:00 p.m. in the spring and fall. It is
closed Thanksgiving, Christmas, and New Year's Day.

Just outside the entrance to the Navy Yard you can see
a multimedia re-creation of the battle of Bunker Hill at
The Bunker Hill Pavilion. Reenactments are shown
every half hour, and the pavilion is open daily from
9:30 a.m. to 4:00 p.m. Admission is $3 for adults, $1.50
for children ages 5 and up, $8 for families. Then, walk up
the hill to the 220-foot-tall **Bunker Hill Monument** that
commemorates the major Revolutionary War battle. The
monument is open from 9:30 a.m. to 6:00 p.m. June

through August, from 9:30 a.m. to 4:00 p.m. September through May. Entrance to the monument is free.

As an alternative to retracing your steps to Faneuil Hall Marketplace on the Freedom Trail, MBTA buses run frequently from Charlestown to downtown Boston and the Faneuil Hall area, letting you save your energy for a stroll through the market.

Lodging

Cosmopolitan city that it is, Boston has plenty of high class hotels to bathe you in luxury. The **Meridien** (617-451-1900) in the financial district has one of the better restaurants in the city—**Julien's**. Doubles start at $220. The **Bostonian** (1-800-343-0922), adjacent to Quincy Market and Haymarket, and a short walk from the North End, has one of the best locations in the city for sightseeing. Doubles range from $230 to $250. **The Ritz-Carlton** (1-800-241-3333) overlooking the Public Gardens is where visiting heads of state stay. Doubles are $235 to $365. The **Four Seasons** (1-800-332-3442) is also adjacent to the Public Gardens, and doubles start at $160 on the weekends and run to $355 for a deluxe room during the week. The **Copley Plaza** (617-267-5300) has one of the most sumptuous lobbies in Boston and is conveniently located in Copley Square. Doubles range from $190 to $250 per night. **The Boston Harbor Hotel** (1-800-752-7077) on the waterfront is an elegant new addition to the Boston lodging scene. Water taxis from the airport stop right at its doorstep. Double rooms with a city view start at $220, and those with a harbor view start at $260. Many of these hotels do have special weekend rates, making them a little more affordable than during the week.

The Lenox Hotel at 710 Boylston Street at Copley Square (617-536-5300 or 1-800-225-7676) and **The Omni Parker House** (617-227-8600 or 1-800-THE-OMNI), which is on the Freedom Trail just a few blocks from Quincy Market, are more reasonably priced than the hotels listed above but are still convenient to sights.

Doubles at the Parker House, which tend to be on the small side, start at $160, while rooms at the Lenox start at $125. Even more of a bargain is the **Howard Johnson's** in Kenmore Square (617-267-3100). For a more homey atmosphere, try **Beacon Hill Bed & Breakfast** at 27 Brimmer Street on the residential "flats" of Beacon Hill near the Charles River. Rooms including breakfast go for $85 to $100 per night (617-523-7376).

Staying in Harvard Square in Cambridge is a pleasant alternative to staying in Boston. There is always something happening in the square, and Boston is an easy subway ride away. **The Charles Hotel** (617-864-1200 or 1-800-882-1818) is the upscale lodging choice with rooms starting at $240, while the **Harvard Manor House** (617-354-7548) across the street offers comfortable accommodations and free parking for about $100 per night.

The Boston International Hostel at 12 Hemenway Street offers dormitory accommodations for only $12 per night. The hostel is close to the Boylston subway stop on the Green Line, to Newbury Street, and to the Prudential Center, and only a five-minute walk from the Museum of Fine Arts. It has a fully equipped kitchen and showers and is handicapped accessible (617-536-2970).

For a more complete listing of hotels in the area, write the **Massachusetts Hotel-Motel Association** at 148 State Street, Suite 400, Boston, MA 02109. They produce a free lodging directory. **Bed & Breakfast Above the Rest** (617-277-2292 or 1-800-677-2262) can help you find a bed and breakfast in the area that's right for your needs. In general, if you are willing to stay outside the city, you'll probably find a wider range of inexpensive hotels but will not have the convenience of the city at your doorstep.

Dining
Boston has no shortage of good restaurants. Four that have stood the test of time are the Locke Ober Cafe, Jacob Wirth's, Durgin Park, and the Union Oyster House. **The**

Locke Ober Cafe (617-542-1340) is down an alley off Winter Street. Established in 1875, it is an old-money institution with dark wood paneling, hard-backed leather chairs, and a men's club atmosphere. Prices are expensive. **Jacob Wirth's** (617-338-8586), across from the New England Medical Center near Chinatown, has changed little in the last 100 years. The wooden floors are well worn, the home-brewed beer (both light and dark) is full-bodied, the hearty meals have a German flavor, and prices are moderate. **Durgin Park** (617-266-1964) in Faneuil Hall Marketplace is yet another Boston tradition, noted for New England-style meals, large portions, and surly waitresses. The restaurant originally served the men who worked the docks (big meals at low prices) and has tried to retain the same atmosphere, although prices are no longer dirt cheap. Just around the corner, **The Union Oyster House** (617-227-2750) has a raw oyster bar and serves the best seafood in town. The restaurant was established in 1826. Entrées range from $15 to $25.

Anthony's Pier 4 at 140 Atlantic Avenue overlooking the harbor and Boston serves seafood on a grand scale. In size, Anthony's is more like a factory than a restaurant, yet it manages to maintain a pleasant atmosphere. Tasty dishes from the sea come with freshly baked popovers, and if you have room for dessert, the baked Alaska is sure to please. Try to get a seat outdoors in the summer. Call (617) 423-6363 for reservations. The **Boston Sail Loft** at 80 Atlantic Avenue also specializes in seafood and overlooks the water but in a crowded yet relaxed milieu. The Sail Loft's menu includes sandwiches, chowder, salads, and pub fare at moderate prices. About a five-minute walk from Faneuil Hall, it is a popular night spot with local young professionals. Even more casual and crowded is **No Name** in the wharf area of the waterfront. What it lacks in ambience, No Name makes up for in low prices and the freshness of their seafood. Call (617) 338-7539 for directions since the restaurant is hard to find, and be prepared to wait on line. They do not take reservations. **Legal Seafoods** in the Boston Park Plaza hotel is also known for its seafaring cuisine (617-426-4444).

You'll be able to get fresh fish most anywhere on this trip. What you won't find elsewhere in New England is the variety of excellent ethnic restaurants that Boston has to offer. Try several of them while you're here. There are two **King & I** restaurants in Boston, at 259 Newbury Street (617-437-9611) and at 145 Charles Street on Beacon Hill (617-227-3320). Both have the same menu offering delicious Thai cuisine, with dinner entrées averaging $9, and lunch entrées $5.50. The spicy aroma of **Kebab n'Kurry**, at Massachusetts Avenue and Beacon Street, can easily entice you into ordering more than you can possibly eat, and everything you sample will be delectable. The basement Indian restaurant is casual and affordably priced at $8.95 to $10.95. Call 617-536-9835. **Casa Romero** specializes in gourmet Mexican and south-western dishes. The restaurant, located in the alley just off Gloucester and Newbury streets, is open Monday through Saturday. Reservations are recommended since the chef's talents are renowned in the area (617-536-4341). Dinner entrées are $10 to $16.

The North End is the place to go for Italian cuisine. **Felicia's** (617-523-9885) and **Villa Francesca** (617-367-2948) on Richmond Street are somewhat expensive, but the food, particularly at Francesca's, lives up to its price. **La Piccola Venezia** (617-523-9802) at 63 Salem Street serves traditional Italian specialties such as cannelloni, manicotti, veal parigina, and lasagna in an informal setting. The menu is written on chalkboards throughout the tiny restaurant. Lunch or dinner for two will be in the $20 range; bring a hearty appetite as the portions are huge! It is not unusual to see a line of people waiting outside on weekend nights since they do not take reservations. If you visit Boston during the summer you may be lucky enough to come upon one of the North End's Italian festivals. You can literally eat your way through the streets! Call (617) 536-4100 for festival information.

Chinatown has a wide selection of Oriental restaurants, enough so that you can walk down the street and eat at whichever one appeals to you the most. Although I've never had a bad meal in Chinatown, my favorite is the

Lucky Dragon at 45 Beach Street. For a spicy inexpensive lunch, two people can share a single generous portion of their Singapore noodles (617-542-0772).

Ice Cream

As cold as the region gets in the winter, oddly enough New England has the highest per capita consumption of ice cream in the country. New Englanders are passionate about their ice cream! Almost every town on the itinerary has at least one ice cream parlor. You will be able to locate them easily by the trail of eagerly slurping patrons. Bostonians are connoisseurs; hence a number of locally famous rival parlors vie for business. Wherever you decide to sample the sweet frozen dessert, you're bound to be pleased.

  Steve's, possibly the best known of the lot, has locations throughout the area including Quincy Market, Downtown Crossing, and on Massachusetts Avenue in Back Bay. Try their mix-ins. Crushed Oreos, Heath bars, chocolate chips, and the like, are hand-blended into fresh ice cream made the old-fashioned way. Their hot fudge sundaes are amazing. Steve Herrell, who originally founded Steve's and later sold the company, is back with his own parlor, **Herrell's,** on Dunster Street in Cambridge. **Emack & Bolio's** on upper Newbury Street also turns out a good product. For basic family-style ice cream, **Brigham's** operates several restaurants in the city. **Il Dolce Momento** on Charles Street in Beacon Hill serves a range of unique Italian gelati flavors and sorbets. This parlor also offers tasty pastries and sandwiches (such as chicken salad with artichoke hearts).

Boston Shopping

Boston shopping affords enough variety so that any visitor should be able to find what he or she is looking for. The best shopping is clustered in five different sections of the city.

  Newbury Street—This handsome street in the heart of Back Bay runs from the edge of the Public Gardens to Massachusetts Avenue and is home to the city's chic boutiques and art galleries. Sumptuous shops range from the trendy to antiques and traditional favorites such as Burberry's and Laura Ashley. You can find several interesting second-hand clothing stores toward the Massachusetts Avenue end of the street. Along the way are plenty of sidewalk cafés catering to weary shoppers. Pucker Safrai Gallery, the Copley Society, and the Victor Hugo Bookshop at number 339 are among my favorite stops on Newbury Street.

Copley Place—This high-class shopping mall is an example of Boston's recent revitalization and gentrification. The Westin and Marriott hotels are at opposite ends of the mall. Tiffany's, Neiman Marcus, and Gucci's are all located here, as well as an excellent newsstand carrying a wide variety of American and continental magazines, a six-cinema movie complex that features the excellent "Where's Boston" documentary film on one screen, and a Rizzoli's bookstore. Saks Fifth Avenue and Lord & Taylor are nearby at the Prudential Center.

Downtown Crossing—This is the area of Washington Street one block east of Park Street station. Though not a visually appealing place to shop, the "World Famous Filene's Basement" is worth a stop, especially for bargain hunters. Barnes and Noble operates a large bookstore here, and fast-food addicts can have their fill at either "The Corner" or the fast-food hall upstairs at Lafayette Place.

Quincy Market—The market is a good place to browse after sightseeing, since many of the stores are open until 9:00 p.m. The specialty carts adjacent to the food hall sell everything from Celtics souvenir shirts to batik sarongs.

Haymarket—This open-air fruit and vegetable market is held every Friday and Saturday alongside Interstate 93 between Quincy Market and the North End. Many of the vendors are true characters, and the market is a ritual that has remained unchanged through the years. You can get a hunk of Brie cheese for a buck, and you may want to load up on fresh fruit and nuts for the trip. Beware: some vendors display gorgeous merchandise at rock bottom

prices but fill your bag with overripe fruit from the back
of the pile. Make sure you pick what you want before you
hand over the money. The best selection is in the morning, while the best prices are at the end of the day when
the vendors try to unload their wares rather than carry
them home.

Nightlife
If you're in a bar-hopping mood, the Quincy Market area
is the best place to start because of the high concentra-
tion of drinking establishments there. **Lord Bunbury's**
tries to capture the flavor of an English pub and draws a
young, boisterous crowd. **Houlihan's** is primarily a restaurant but has a dance floor that packs them in after
dinner. **Cricket's** attracts the business-suit set, and
Lily's has a piano bar and outdoor seating and is a great
place to people-watch on hot summer nights. Near
Faneuil Hall, **The Black Rose** is a lively Irish pub and *the*
place to go on St. Patrick's Day, if you can get in.

Back Bay has a number of popular night spots including **Friday's** on Newbury Street which has a fun menu,
tasty appetizers, and a crowded bar area to mix and mingle.
Daisy Buchanan's, also on Newbury Street, used to be a
Red Sox hangout but is now dominated by swinging sin-
gles. **The Elliot Lounge,** on Massachusetts and
Commonwealth avenues, sports a relaxed and casual
atmosphere. This is where the runners flock after com-
pleting the Boston Marathon. **The Top of the Hub** atop
the Prudential building has a terrific view of the city. The
drinks aren't cheap, but the view is worth it. If your tastes
run to Broadway show tunes, try **Diamond Jim's** piano
bar at the Lenox Hotel. Patrons are welcome to stand up
and try their hand at a song or two.

On Beacon Hill one of my favorites is **The Seven's
Pub** at 77 Charles Street. They serve great sandwiches
with homemade potato salad at rock bottom prices and
have a good selection of imported beer. The milieu is
smoky and very casual. The clientele is mixed but always
friendly. Several blocks away on Beacon Street, **The Bull**

n' Finch Pub inspired the TV sitcom "Cheers." Although it has lost some of its neighborhood appeal to fame, it is still a fun place to go, especially if you are a fan of the show. For more elegant sipping, try upstairs in the lounge at **The Hampshire House**.

Landsdowne Street, across from Fenway Park, is lined with nightclubs that generally cater to a young crowd, the most popular being **Venus de Milo**. If you like rock-and-roll, you'll have to travel to the **Channel Club** at 25 Necco Street in the Ford Point area of Boston below South Station. Live bands perform there regularly.

Other

If a foreigner walks up to you on the streets of Boston and asks you "where is this place that you have war," they are probably not referring to the Bunker Hill Monument but to an area known locally as the "Combat Zone." The Zone lies between the theater district and Chinatown and is comparable to New York City's Times Square district. Although the Zone is shrinking, what remains is a strip of X-rated movie houses and is best avoided.

The Performing Arts

Music lovers should not miss the world-famous **Boston Pops** directed by respected composer John Williams or the **Boston Symphony Orchestra's** more traditional classical performances. Both make their home in Symphony Hall, except during the summer when the BSO travels to Tanglewood and the Pops give their annual Fourth of July concert at the Esplanade on the Charles River. Call (617) 266-1492 for ticket information. Boston also has its own ballet company, **The Boston Ballet.** Call (617) 542-1323 for their schedule. Annual performances of *The Nutcracker* are a holiday favorite.

The **BOSTIX** booth in Faneuil Hall Marketplace sells tickets for all major theatrical productions. Check with them to see what's in town during your visit. It is sometimes possible to get reduced ticket prices there the day of performance. Call (617) 723-5181 for up-to-date schedule and ticket information.

Sports
If you enjoy a good game of baseball, you'll especially appreciate watching one in **Fenway Park**, home of the **Boston Red Sox**. The ballpark's relatively small size makes attending a game more a participatory than a spectator sport. Call (617) 267-8661 for schedule and ticket information.

Wintertime visitors can catch either the **Boston Celtics** or **Boston Bruins** at the **Boston Garden.** Call (617) 227-3200 for the Garden's schedule and ticket information.

Racing buffs will be drawn to **Suffolk Downs** for horse racing and **Wonderland** for dog racing. Both tracks have their own stops on the Blue Line subway.

BOSTON'S MUSEUMS

The scope of Boston's museums is tremendous, from ancient Egyptian art to state-of-the-art computers, from an authentic Japanese house to lightning demonstrations, and from dolphins to European tapestries. Today you'll have a chance to uncover past civilizations and look into our own future.

Suggested Schedule

8:30 a.m.	Breakfast.
9:30 a.m.	Spend the morning exploring your choice of museums along the waterfront.
12:30 p.m.	Lunch in Chinatown.
1:30 p.m.	Visit the Boston Museum of Fine Arts.
4:00 p.m.	Visit the Isabella Stewart Gardner Museum.
Sunset	After dinner in Back Bay, visit the John Hancock Observation Deck or the Prudential's Skywalk to watch the sun set.

Sightseeing Highlights

▲**Boston Tea Party Ship & Museum**—You get to throw a tea chest overboard in protest of the British tax on this replica of the eighteenth-century ship where the famous revolt originally took place. (The chests aren't actually filled with tea and are connected by rope, but at least you get to feel like a rebel.) The museum is open daily from 9:00 a.m. to dusk except for Thanksgiving, Christmas, and New Year's Day. It is located at 300 Congress Street on Museum Wharf and admission is charged.

▲**Boston Children's Museum** (▲▲▲ If you are traveling with children)—The museum is known for its "hands-on" exhibits, Native American collection, and Japanese home painstakingly moved here piece by piece from Kyoto. Children magically become hushed when they enter the Japanese house, but in the rest of the museum laughter prevails as they try on clothes in Grand-

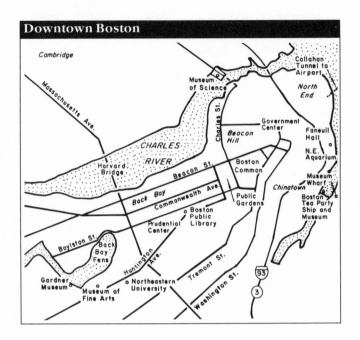

Downtown Boston

mother's Attic, scramble up and down over several levels in the climbing structure, and blow bubbles as big as they are. Teens will enjoy "faultless jamming," in the clubhouse designed especially for them, with electronic musical instruments that sound good together no matter how they are played. The museum is open daily from 10:00 a.m. to 5:00 p.m., Friday evening until 9:00 p.m., and is closed Monday from Labor Day through June. Admission is $6 for adults, $5 for seniors and children ages 2 to 15, $1 for one-year-olds. Admission Friday evenings from 5:00 p.m. to 9:00 p.m. is only $1 for everyone. The museum is located on Congress Street at Museum Wharf.

▲▲**The Computer Museum**—With the influence of the high-tech industry in Boston and nearby Massachusetts Institute of Technology turning out computer geniuses of the future, it is no wonder that Boston has the first museum devoted to the history of the computer. Get a close-up look at the first computers, then test your skills in the PC gallery. On Museum Wharf next to the Children's

Museum, the Computer Museum is open daily 10:00 a.m.
to 5:00 p.m., Friday evening until 9:00 p.m.; closed on
Monday during the winter months. Admission is $6 for
adults, $5 for students and seniors, children under 5 free.
Admission is half-price on Friday evenings.

▲▲ **New England Aquarium**—What trip to the coast
would be complete without a look at the inhabitants of
the sea? The aquarium has a magnificent cylindrical glass
tank several stories high. You can views hundreds of species of sea life including sharks, barracudas, and giant sea
turtles as you wind down the spiral ramp. Dolphin shows
are included in your admission. If you don't have time to
go in the museum, at least take a few minutes to watch the
seals play at the outside entrance to the aquarium as you
stroll along the waterfront. Hours vary depending upon
the season, but the aquarium is generally open daily from
9:00 a.m. to at least 5:00 p.m., later in the summer. Call
(617) 742-8870 for current hours and admission prices.
The aquarium is located on Central Wharf, three blocks
from Faneuil Hall Marketplace next to the Aquarium "T"
stop on the Blue Line.

▲▲ **Boston Museum of Science**—Test your strength,
then discover the power of electricity. Learn about the
earth's gravitational force, then explore faraway planets in
the planetarium. One can spend hours in this fascinating
museum unearthing the secrets of nature's unseen energy
sources, as well as those that are visible to the naked eye,
and see how man tries to tame and control them. Many of
the exhibits are participatory. The museum is open from
9:00 a.m. to 5:00 p.m. Tuesday through Sunday, and Friday evening until 9:00 p.m. Admission is $5 for adults, $3
for children ages 4 to 14. Admission to the Planetarium
and Omni Theater is separate, but combination tickets are
available. The museum has its own subway stop on the
Lechmere branch of the Green Line.

▲▲▲ **Boston Museum of Fine Arts**—This is one of the
most highly respected art museums in the country. The
collection consists of ancient Greek, Roman, Egyptian,
and Oriental art, with classic European and American
artists represented as well. There are also American

period rooms, early American furniture, silver, and fine musical instruments. The West Wing addition, designed by I. M. Pei, houses changing exhibits, an attractive restaurant, and a superlative museum gift shop. Courtyard dining adjoins the lower-level cafeteria. The museum is open Tuesday through Sunday 10:00 a.m. to 4:45 p.m. and Wednesday until 10:45 p.m. The West Wing is open until 9:45 p.m. on Thursday and Friday evenings. Admission is $6 for adults, $5 for seniors and students, $3 for children 6 to 17. Everyone is admitted free of charge on Wednesday from 4:00 p.m. to 6:00 p.m. The museum is located on Huntington Avenue across from Northeastern University. The Huntington Avenue branch of the Green Line stops right in front of the museum.

▲▲ **Isabella Stewart Gardner Museum**—My favorite museum in Boston, this Venetian-style palazzo on the Fenway just two blocks from the Museum of Fine Arts houses Ms. Gardner's extraordinary private collection. Imagine having a chapel in your home with a thirteenth-century stained-glass window and living with not one but three Rembrandts. Ms. Gardner, an avid patron of the arts, made it her life's work to amass this collection ranging from early Italian religious paintings to American and French impressionists of the last century to beautifully intricate European laces. The courtyard, complete with Roman statues and mosaics, is abloom with flowers in every season and makes a splendid haven from the outside world. Concerts are given frequently in one of the halls, usually on Sunday afternoons at 3:00 p.m. There is also a café on the premises. Despite the much-publicized theft of some of the museum's most famous works in 1990, it remains a treasure well worth unearthing. The museum is open Tuesday noon to 6:30 p.m. (until 5:00 p.m. during July and August), and Wednesday through Sunday noon to 5:00 p.m. Admission is $5 for adults, $2.50 for students and senior citizens, and children under 12 are admitted free. There is no admission charge on Wednesday.

▲▲ **The John Hancock Observatory** or **The Skywalk at the Prudential Building**—From the top of the John Hancock Tower in Copley Square, or the Prudential building nearby, you'll see magnificent views of the city and beyond on clear days and the city sparkling as night falls. The Hancock Observatory is open Monday through Saturday 9:00 a.m. to 11:00 p.m., Sunday from 10:00 a.m. to 11:00 p.m., May through October, and noon to 11:00 p.m. November through April (last entry 10:15 p.m.). Admission is $2.75 for adults, $2.00 for seniors and children 5 to 15. The Skywalk at the Prudential building just down the street is not as tall but has views in all directions (the Hancock is closed off on one side) and is slightly less expensive. Admission is $2.50 for adults and $1.50 for seniors and children 5 to 15.

Other Sights
You may wish to seek out any of a number of small museums that cater to special interests. **The Institute of Contemporary Art** at 955 Boylston Street features changing exhibits of contemporary art. The museum is open Wednesday through Sunday from 11:00 a.m. to 5:00 p.m. and until 8:00 p.m. on Thursday and Friday evenings. Admission is charged. **The Museum of Afro-American Artists** focuses on visual arts by black artists. It is located at 300 Walnut Avenue and is generally open Tuesday through Sunday, but hours can vary, so call ahead for information (617-442-8614). Admission is charged. **The Christian Science Center** behind the Prudential building is architecturally interesting, as is **The Boston Public Library** several blocks away in Copley Square. The library was designed by the highly regarded architectural firm of McKim, Mead & White. Another library, **The Boston Athenaeum** at 10½ Beacon Street near the State House, is a long-standing Boston institution. The library's collection includes early American publications and an exhibit gallery of American Art.

   The Black Heritage Trail is similar to the Freedom Trail and highlights significant places in Boston's black history. The **African Meeting House**, the oldest standing black church in the United States, is one of the stops on the trail. The main visitor center is located at 46 Joy

Street, but you can also pick up a trail brochure at the
tourist information center on Boston Common. For an
outdoor excursion, a visit to the **Arnold Arboretum** at the
Arborway in Jamaica Plain, Boston, is well worthwhile—
especially during lilac season. The 265-acre landscaped
Arboretum has over 7,000 varieties of trees (617-524-1718).

Boston has a number of historic homes that can be
toured, including the Victorian **Gibson House Museum**
at 137 Beacon Street in Back Bay. (Tours are given at 2:00,
3:00, and 4:00 p.m. Wednesday through Sunday, May
through October, and November through April on Saturday and Sunday by appointment; call 617-267-6338).
Nichols House Museum, an 1809 period home, is on
Mt. Vernon Street atop Beacon Hill (open Monday,
Wednesday, and Saturday from 1:00 p.m. to 5:00 p.m.;
admission is $3).

Beer lovers may wish to tour one of Boston's breweries.
The **Boston Beer Company** brews local favorite Samuel
Adams Lager and can be toured on Thursday and Saturday
at 2:00 p.m (617-522-9080). The **Massachusetts Bay
Brewing Company** also runs brewery tours on Tuesday,
Friday, and Saturday. Call (617) 574-9551 for information.

Schedule Option
Too many museums for your taste? How about a morning
or afternoon harbor cruise. Most of the cruises leave from
piers near the Aquarium stop on the Blue Line. The cost
depends upon whether you plan to take a short cruise in
the harbor or out to the harbor islands (usually only
several dollars per person) or if you wish to take one
where dinner or live band music is included. Call **Bay
State Cruises**, (617) 723-7800, **Boston Harbor
Cruises**, (617) 227-4321, or **Massachusetts Bay Lines**,
(617) 749-4500, for additional information.

Itinerary Option
If your time in the Boston area permits, modify this
itinerary to add a day trip to one of New England's foremost attractions, **Old Sturbridge Village,** a living

museum that re-creates everyday life in an 1830s New England village. Candle making, blacksmithing, and woodworking are among the craft demonstrations you'll see there. Although children especially enjoy the village, adults will certainly be impressed as well. The village is open daily year-round, except for major holidays and Mondays during the winter months. Admission is high—$14 for adults, $6 for children 6 to 15—but the visit is an all-day event. From Boston, take the Massachusetts Turnpike (Interstate 90) west to Exit 9 and follow signs to the village.

The Sturbridge area is also one of the largest apple growing regions in the state, and many of the orchards have "pick your own" programs, making a Sturbridge outing fun for the whole family, especially on a crisp, clear autumn day. The trip from Boston is about 60 miles each way. If you want to spend the night in Sturbridge, the **Publick House & Country Motor Lodge** is a popular spot. Call (508) 347-3313 for reservations.

CAMBRIDGE

Cambridge, like Boston, has been around for over 350 years. Remarkably, Harvard University has been in existence almost as long, and its influence is felt in just about every aspect of Cambridge life, particularly in bustling Harvard Square.

Suggested Schedule

9:00 a.m.	Travel from Boston to Cambridge.
9:30 a.m.	Spend the morning on the grounds and in the museums of the nation's oldest university, Harvard.
12:00 noon	Lunch.
1:00 p.m.	Walk down Brattle Street as far as Fresh Pond Parkway to view Cambridge's loveliest homes. Visit the home of Henry Wadsworth Longfellow on the return trip.
3:00 p.m.	Spend the rest of the afternoon browsing through Harvard Square's many bookshops and boutiques.
6:00 p.m.	Dinner in Cambridge, then visit an area nightclub.

Travel Route
If you're coming from downtown Boston, take the Red Line on the subway toward Alewife and get off at the Harvard Square stop.

Sightseeing Highlights
▲▲▲ **Harvard University**—This is the oldest university in the United States. Its ivy-covered buildings and quiet courtyards (in some areas of the school) make it one of the prettiest as well. Stop in at Widener Library as you walk through "The Yard"; it has one of the most extensive collections of any library in the country. The library has a small exhibit depicting Cambridge history which may help put the city in perspective.

Harvard's huge endowment has given the school out-standing museums and innumerable buildings of interest. See if you can guess which one was funded by a major camera company (hint: it's near The Yard). **The Fogg Art Museum** (32 Quincy St.), with its fine collection of impressionist works, including a Degas ballerina, and Romanesque and medieval works, is my favorite Harvard museum. At **The Busch Reisinger** (29 Kirkland St.) the specialty is German expressionism. **The Sackler** (Quincy St. and Broadway), the newest of the Harvard museums, concentrates on Far Eastern and Islamic works of art. An admission charge of $4 will admit you to all three museums. They are open Tuesday through Sunday 10:00 a.m. to 5:00 p.m.

Also operated by Harvard are the **Botanical Museum** with its unusual glass flowers exhibit, the **Peabody Museum of Archaeology and Ethnology**, the **Museum of Comparative Zoology**, the **Mineralogical and Geological Museum,** and the **Semitic Museum.** These museums are located on Oxford Street and Divinity Avenue. The Semitic Museum is open Monday through Friday 11:00 a.m. to 5:00 p.m., Sunday 1:00 p.m. to 5:00 p.m. The others (all housed in the same building) are open Monday through Saturday 9:00 a.m. to 4:15 p.m., Sunday from 1:00 p.m. to 4:15 p.m.; admission is $3 for adults, $2 for seniors and students, $1 for children 5 to 15. Call (617) 495-1910 for additional information.

▲▲ **Longfellow National Historic Site**—This was the home of poet Henry Wadsworth Longfellow for 45 years until his death in 1882. His major works were written here, among them *Hiawatha* and *Evangeline.* The house, built in 1759, has additional historic significance as George Washington's headquarters during the siege of Boston in 1776. It is open daily except for Thanksgiving, Christmas, and New Year's Day and is just one of many beautiful homes along Brattle Street. Admission is charged.

▲ **MIT Museum**—In addition to exhibits on holography, engineering, science, and architecture—exhibits you'd expect from a university that has produced some of the

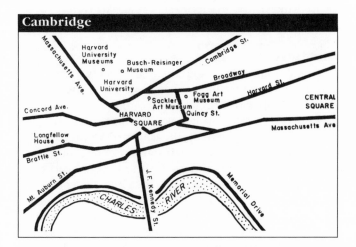

world's greatest scientific minds—this museum also has an art collection and a model ship gallery. The main museum is located at 265 Massachusetts Avenue near Central Square and is open Tuesday through Friday from 9:00 a.m. to 5:00 p.m., and on weekends from 1:00 p.m. to 5:00 p.m. The Compton Gallery is in building 10 of the school's main campus (open Monday through Friday 9:00 a.m. to 5:00 p.m.), and the Hart Nautical Galleries are in building 5 (open daily 9:00 a.m. to 8:00 p.m.).

▲ **Mount Auburn Cemetery**—This is one of the most beautifully landscaped urban cemeteries anywhere. There's even a small lookout tower where you can view the surrounding cities of Cambridge and Boston. Charles Bullfinch (the architect who designed the State House), American artist Winslow Homer, Henry Wadsworth Longfellow, and Oliver Wendell Holmes are all buried here. At 580 Mt. Auburn Street, it is a bit of a walk from Harvard Square but may be worthwhile if you appreciate historic tombstones.

Helpful Hints

The Cambridge Discovery Booth next to the "T" station in Harvard Square sells historic walking tour maps of the area for $1. The booth is open 9:00 a.m. to 5:00 p.m. Monday through Saturday, 1:00 p.m. to 5:00 p.m. on Sunday mid-June through Labor Day, on weekends only through October. Call (617) 497-1630 for information.

Cambridge Shopping
Because of its proximity to Harvard University, Harvard Square has more than its share of bookstores. **The Coop** (Harvard Cooperative Society), Harvard University's main bookstore, also has considerable record and art print departments. **Wordsworth**, the **Harvard Square Bookstore**, and **Reading International** can all be found in and around the square. You can browse to your heart's content, since most are open late. It's a book lover's dream! When you run out of bookstores, there are plenty of clothing stores and specialty shops, particularly in the **Galleria** and **Charles Hotel** shopping complexes, to keep even the most determined shopper busy for hours. Don't miss the newsstand in the center of Harvard Square: its selection of magazines and newspapers is endless.

Dining
Harvard Square's restaurants run the gamut from fast-food establishments to upscale bistros. **The Wursthaus** on JFK Street serves excellent lox, bagels, and cream cheese, cold-cut platters, and a marvelous selection of beers from around the world. Try **Yenching** on Massachusetts Avenue near the "T" station for good Chinese food at moderate prices. **Au Bon Pain,** next to Yenching, is the place to people-watch at outdoor tables. Study chess players intent on their game as you sample croissants in every flavor imaginable, gourmet sandwiches such as tarragon chicken or chicken with bernaise, and creamy soups from Au Bon Pain's kitchen for as little as $3.50 per meal. **Grendel's Den** (617-491-1160), at JFK and Winthrop streets, has a terrific salad bar, good Greek combo plates, and a pleasant atmosphere. Prices start around $6.

   The Garage on the corner of Mt. Auburn, JFK, and Dunster streets is filled with out-of-the-ordinary fast-food restaurants. **Fromaggio's** creates unique sandwiches with fillings such as ratatouille and boursin cheese on fresh homemade bread. At **Baby Watson's** chocoholics must try the "chocolate orgasms"; the cheesecake is also pretty irresistible. **Cafe Aventura** serves great pizza for a song. **Leo's Place**, across the street from the Garage, offers the best basic Swiss burger and fries around.

At the other end of the spectrum is **Upstairs at the Pudding** (617-864-1933) for fine dining. The "Pudding" is at 10 Holyoke Street, reservations are recommended, and meals are expensive. Two restaurants outside of Harvard Square that really let you experience other cultures are **The Averof** (617-354-4500) in Porter Square and **Cantares** (617-547-6300) in Inman Square. Both have fine food. The Averof specializes in Greek food, while Cantares serves Spanish and Latin American fare. Belly dancers perform at the Averof, and live Latin American bands play at Cantares.

Nightlife

Ryles Jazz Club in Inman Square has long been recognized as one of the Boston area's best jazz bars (617-876-9330). The **Regattabar** at the Charles Hotel in Harvard Square also has live jazz most evenings. The **Brattle Theatre** (617-876-6837) on Brattle Street in Harvard Square shows current art films, revives old film classics, and occasionally runs film festivals.

CONCORD AND LEXINGTON

The first shot in the Revolutionary War was fired in Concord on April 19, 1775. During the hundred years that followed, Concord was also home to some of America's foremost literary figures — Ralph Waldo Emerson, Nathaniel Hawthorne, Louisa May Alcott, and Henry David Thoreau. As a result of Thoreau's strong naturalist influence, parts of Concord have been set aside as nature preserves. Today you'll see what inspired writers to live in Concord. Then visit neighboring Lexington, which also has its share of charm and history.

Suggested Schedule

8:00 a.m.	Breakfast.
8:30 a.m.	Leave for Concord.
9:00 a.m.	Visit the historic North Bridge, Sleepy Hollow Cemetery, and Great Meadows Wildlife Refuge.
11:00 a.m.	Tour the Concord Museum.
12:00 noon	Drive to Walden Pond for a midday hike, swim, and picnic lunch.
2:00 p.m.	Visit the Old Manse, Orchard House, Emerson's House, or the Thoreau Lyceum.
3:00 p.m.	Travel to Lexington to visit the Museum of Our National Heritage.
4:30 p.m.	Leave for Salem.
5:30 p.m.	Check into accommodations.

Travel Route: Boston to Concord to Salem (60 miles)
From Boston, take Storrow Drive west following signs to Fresh Pond Parkway and Arlington. Get on Fresh Pond Parkway and follow signs to Route 2. The entrance to Route 2 is two-thirds of the way around the second rotary.

If this is your first experience with rotaries, a word of caution: these circular intersections often found in Massachusetts when three or more roads come together, can be dangerous, so approach them carefully. A Massachusetts driver's approach to rotaries is, "Close your eyes and go." While this is not recommended, neither is timidity. Many unaccustomed drivers get hit because they hesitate too long. Try to blend into rotary traffic as easily as possible, moving at a slow but steady speed. Do not stop in the middle of a rotary! If you miss your exit, just continue on around and exit on your next circuit.

Once on Route 2 west, it's about a 15-minute drive to Concord. Follow signs to Concord center. There is a tourist information booth on your left as you approach the center.

From Concord, take Route 2A east to Lexington. You will cross Interstate 95/Route 128 before reaching the Museum of Our National Heritage. You may want to pick up fresh fruit for the trip at one of the roadside farm stands along the route.

From Lexington, take Interstate 95/Route 128 north toward Gloucester. I-95 splits off from Route 128 at Wakefield. Stay on Route 128 to Exit 35E, Route 114 east for Salem. The Lexington and Salem exits are approximately 20 miles apart. Should you wish to stay in Marblehead for the night, continue on Route 114 east from Salem for 5 miles, then follow signs to Marblehead Center.

Sightseeing Highlights
▲▲▲The North Bridge—On this site, British and Revolutionary troops first clashed. Visit the bridge more for its historical significance than for what you'll see here today. The Minute Man statue now stands at the site in memory of that fateful battle. The statue was sculpted by Daniel Chester French, whose grave is in nearby Sleepy Hollow Cemetery and whose home and studio you'll visit later in the trip. The visitor center on the hill above the bridge houses a gift shop and replicas of military attire that the minutemen used. The bridge is on Monument Street about ¾-mile from the center of Concord. There is no admission fee.
▲Sleepy Hollow Cemetery—As you travel back toward Concord center from the North Bridge, turn left

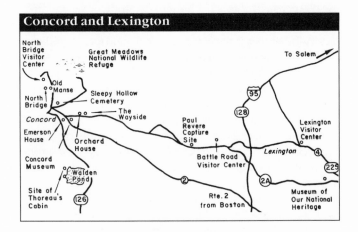

Concord and Lexington

onto Bedford Street. The entrance to the cemetery will
be on your left. Follow signs to Author's Ridge. Ralph
Waldo Emerson, Henry David Thoreau, Nathaniel Hawthorne, Louisa May Alcott, and sculptor Daniel Chester
French are all buried here.

▲**Great Meadows Wildlife Refuge**—This marshy area
was frequented by Thoreau in his study of nature. Today
you can follow the 1¾-mile Dike Trail loop and perhaps
see a fox, muskrat, or weasel in addition to the various
species of waterfowl that nest in the wetlands. To get
there from the cemetery, continue on Bedford Road for
about ¾-mile, then turn left onto Monsen Road. Stay on
Monsen Road to the refuge entrance.

▲▲**Concord Museum**—The museum brings together
Concord's military and literary histories. Items of interest
on the museum tour include Paul Revere's lantern, which
hung in the Old North Church in Boston the night of his
famous ride, and personal articles of Henry David Thoreau
and Ralph Waldo Emerson, who were friends as well as
fellow writers. The museum is open from 10:00 a.m. to
4:00 p.m. Monday through Saturday, and from 1:00 p.m.
to 4:00 p.m. Sunday. It is closed on major holidays.
Admission is $5 for adults, $4 for seniors, $3 for students,
$1.50 for children. The museum is at 200 Lexington
Road, just east of the intersection of Routes 2 and 2A.

▲**Walden Pond**—Henry David Thoreau's famous retreat from "civilization" is now a popular escape for Boston city dwellers and their suburban counterparts. Being relatively mud-free compared to most ponds, and much warmer than the Atlantic, Walden Pond is a preferred place to swim in the area. The pond can get crowded on a hot summer day, but the farther you walk from the main beach, the better chance you have of finding a secluded pond-side picnic spot. There is a model of Thoreau's house next to the parking lot, and the actual house site is about a ten-minute walk in from Route 126. There is a charge for the parking lot, and it is the only legal spot to park within walking distance. To get to the pond, follow Walden Street from Concord center south for about a mile. You will cross Route 2, and the pond will be on your right, the parking lot on your left.

▲**The Old Manse**—On Monument Street just below the North Bridge, the Old Manse was built in 1770 and was, at different times, home to both Emerson and Nathaniel Hawthorne. The house is open seasonally. Call (508) 369-3909 for hours of operation. Admission is $3.50 for adults, $2.50 for senior citizens, $1.50 for children 6 to 16.

▲**Orchard House**—This was the home of Louisa May Alcott from 1858 to 1877 and the setting for her famous novel, *Little Women*. Many actual furnishings are on display, including sketches done by an Alcott sister which still remain on one of the bedroom walls. The chapel in back of the house was built in 1884 to house meetings of the Concord School of Philosophy. The school was founded by A. Bronson Alcott, Louisa's father. The house is open for tours April through October 10:00 a.m. to 4:30 p.m. Monday through Saturday, Sundays and holidays from 1:00 p.m. to 4:30 p.m. Admission is $4 for adults, $3 for senior citizens, $2 for children 6 to 17. The house is on Route 2A (Lexington Road) going toward Lexington.

▲**Emerson's House**—Ralph Waldo Emerson lived here for almost 50 years until his death in 1882. Many of the writer's personal artifacts are on display, including a desk

he used and part of his personal library. On Cambridge
Turnpike just across from the Concord Museum, the
house is open from mid-April through mid-October,
Thursday through Saturday from 10:00 a.m. to 4:30 p.m.,
Sunday from 2:00 p.m. to 4:30 p.m. Admission is
charged.

▲**Thoreau Lyceum**—At 156 Belknap Street, the Lyceum
is filled with Thoreau memorabilia and includes a bookshop and library specializing in Thoreau's works and a
replica of his house at Walden Pond. The Lyceum is open
from 10:00 a.m. to 5:00 p.m. daily April through December, 2:00 p.m. to 5:00 p.m. on Sunday. It is closed during
January but open weekends during February and March.
Admission is $2 for adults, $1.50 for students, $.50 for
children under 12.

▲**The Wayside**—Louisa May Alcott and Nathaniel Hawthorne both lived in this nineteenth-century home. The
house is open seasonally, and admission is charged. Call
(508) 369-6975 for hours it is open during your visit.

▲**Museum of Our National Heritage**—The museum
is devoted to preserving and showing all facets of
America's heritage through changing exhibits that range
from antique quilts to decorative arts to early military
paraphernalia. It is open year-round, Monday through
Saturday 10:00 a.m. to 5:00 p.m., Sunday noon to 5:00 p.m.,
closing only for Thanksgiving, Christmas, and New Year's
Day. Admission is free. The museum is located at 33 Mar-
rett Road on Route 2A in Lexington.

Lodging

In Salem, the following inn establishments are all close to
the main tourist attractions. **The Salem Inn** at 7 Summer
Street is in an attractive old brick building, diagonally
across from the Witch House. Double rooms and suites
run from $80 to $95 (508-741-0680 or 1-800-446-2995).
The Hawthorne Hotel, an elegant small hotel on the
town common, keeps company with Salem's stateliest
homes. Doubles start at $80 per night (508-744-4080).
The Stepping Stone Inn (508-741-8900), adjacent to

the Witch Museum at 19 Washington Square, is a cozy bed
and breakfast with a cheery breakfast room and central
location ($75-$125 including full breakfast). The Salem
Inn and Hawthorne Hotel both have decent restaurants as
well.

Although you will be spending a full day exploring
Salem tomorrow, and the accommodations listed above
are convenient to sights, you may wish to travel 6 miles
farther to the charming seaside town of Marblehead for
lodging tonight and tomorrow night. A stroll down its
winding streets, a seafood dinner overlooking the water,
and a drive out onto affluent Marblehead Neck are all
excellent ways to relax after a busy day of sightseeing.
Two bed and breakfasts that overlook the ocean are
Spray Cliff (make reservations through the Salem Inn,
508-741-0680) at 25 Spray Avenue and **Harborside
House** (617-631-1032) at 23 Gregory Street. Both offer
continental breakfast but only a few rooms, so reservations are wise. Rooms at the Spray Cliff run from $95 to
$200, while Harborside House is somewhat less expen-
sive. **10 Mugford Street** is also a pleasant bed and breakfast that serves a buffet-style breakfast in the morning.
Double rooms are $75, and a two-room suite with a pri-
vate bath is $95. Call (617) 639-0343 for reservations. **The
Brimblecomb Hill Bed & Breakfast** across the street
is also convenient to downtown Marblehead; doubles
range from $60 to $70 per night (617-631-3172).

Camping
There are campsites at **Winter Island Maritime Park** at
50 Winter Island Road in Salem. Sites are $10 to $12, and
the campground is open May through early October.
A trolley stops at the campground and will take you to
Salem's historic sights. Call (508) 745-9430 for information.

Dining
In Salem, **Pickering Wharf** has the highest concentra-
tion of restaurants, generally fast-food and take-out oper-

ations ranging from Chinese to pizza. **Victoria Station**
(508-745-3400), at Pickering Wharf on the water, has outdoor seating in summer and good steak and seafood
dinner entrées that run from $10.95 to $16.95. Lunch
prices start around $5. **The Chase Restaurant**
(508-744-0000) also at Pickering Wharf is a popular
Salem dining spot.

In Marblehead, **Rosalie's** at 18 Sewall Street is the
place to go. Rosalie's delicious northern Italian cuisine is
generally considered to be the best Italian food north of
Boston. Entrées range in price from the low to high teens,
and reservations are a must (617-631-5353). **Danielle's
Café** downstairs, named for Rosalie's daughter, serves
northern Italian cuisine in a festive setting. All entrées are
under $10. **The Barnacle** (617-631-4236) and **The
Landing** (617-631-1878) both overlook Marblehead harbor and serve fresh seafood. Prices are moderate to
expensive. **The King's Rook** at 12 State Street is a cozy
coffeehouse that serves copious salads and tasty desserts
(617-631-9838). Chocolate lovers must find their way to
Stowaway Sweets candy shop at 154 Atlantic Avenue.
The "chocolate meltaways" are positively out of this
world (617-631-0303).

SALEM

Salem is both beguiling and bewitching. It is a small city struggling to preserve its past glory while striving to keep pace with the twentieth century. The infamous witch trials of 1692 took place in Salem, and the House of Seven Gables immortalized by Hawthorne is here. Fewer people know about Salem's prominence in early America's foreign trade network. Today we'll examine all three facets of Salem's past.

Suggested Schedule

9:00 a.m.	Breakfast, then stroll past beautiful Federalist homes on Washington Square surrounding the Salem Common.
10:00 a.m.	Visit the Salem Witch Museum.
11:00 a.m.	Visit the Peabody Museum.
1:00 p.m.	Lunch.
2:00 p.m.	Spend midafternoon touring Essex Institute, the Witch House, a historic home, or just window-shopping.
4:00 p.m.	End your day in Salem with a visit to the House of Seven Gables.

Travel Route
Most of the day will be spent on foot. Use caution when driving in Salem's center. There is at least one intersection where as many as six roads come together without so much as a stoplight, stop sign, or yield sign. The last time I was there, the most courteous driver in the intersection was a taxi driver.

Sightseeing Highlights
Salem—In 1692, mass hysteria gripped the city of Salem when several girls were said to have been bewitched by a West Indian servant named Tituba. This started a rash of accusations, and just about anyone exhibiting strange behavior was said to be a witch. More than two hundred

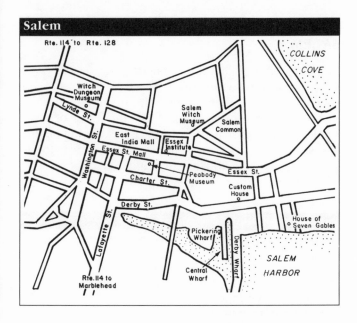

townsfolk in all were arrested for allegedly practicing witchcraft. Nineteen of the accused were hung before Massachusetts Governor William Phipps put a stop to the executions in 1693. However, the events of 1692 were so traumatic that Salem is known, even today, as the "witch city."

▲▲The Salem Witch Museum—On Salem Common, the museum houses an audiovisual presentation of the events of 1692. It is an entertaining introduction to the history of the witch trials. The museum is open daily from 10:00 a.m. to 5:00 p.m., to 7:00 p.m. during July and August. Admission is $3.50 for adults, $3 for seniors, and $2 for children 6 to 14. The presentation is shown on the hour and half hour.

▲The Witch House—On the corner of Essex and Washington streets, this building is known as the witch house because those accused of being witches were interrogated here by Judge Jonathan Corwin before going to trial. Built around 1642, it is one of the oldest houses still standing in the United States. Tour guides explain uses of eighteenth-century everyday household items and how expressions such as "sleep tight" and "turning the tables" originally came into our language. Admission is $3 for adults, $1.50 for children 5 to 16. The house is open seasonally from mid-March through November 10:00 a.m. to 4:30 p.m., to 6:00 p.m. during July and August.

▲**The Witches Dungeon**—The trial of Sarah Goode, one of the accused witches, is reenacted at the Dungeon at 16 Lynde Street in a re-creation of the dungeon where alleged witches awaited hanging. Open daily from 10:00 a.m. to 5:00 p.m. May through November. Admission is $3.50 for adults, $2 for children 6 to 14.

▲▲**Essex Institute**—At 132 Essex Street, the institute consists of a museum building containing a collection of art, silver, dolls, toys, and military artifacts from Essex county and four period homes, the oldest dating from 1684. The institute operates special witchcraft and Salem history tours during the summer. The last tour of the day leaves at 3:30 p.m. The museum is open Monday through Saturday 9:00 a.m. to 5:00 p.m., Sundays and holidays 1:00 to 5:00 p.m.; closed Mondays November through May. The admission charge varies depending whether you visit only the museum or also tour one or more of the historic houses.

▲▲▲**The Peabody Museum**—On East India Square at Liberty and Essex streets, the Peabody is a gem, with extraordinary depth for a small city museum. There are exhibits of nautical paintings and instruments and ships' figureheads, as one might expect in a city whose livelihood came from the sea. However, the most fascinating exhibits are those devoted to goods brought back to this country through foreign trade. The collection includes fine china from the Orient, tribal artifacts from the Pacific islands, exotic furniture, silver, and even a miniature Taj Mahal carved in ivory. For children, there are several rooms devoted to natural history. The museum is open Monday through Saturday 10:00 a.m. to 5:00 p.m., Sunday noon to 5:00 p.m. Admission is $5 for adults, $4 for senior citizens and students, $2.50 for children 6 to 12.

▲**Salem Maritime National Historic Site**—Run by

the National Park Service at 174 Derby Street, the site includes the Custom and Derby houses along with several wharves and warehouses illustrating Salem's former dominance as a port. It is open daily September through June 8:30 a.m. to 5:00 p.m., and July 1 through Labor Day 8:30 a.m. to 6:00 p.m. Admission is free.

▲▲**The House of Seven Gables**—At 54 Turner Street on the water, this is the house that inspired Nathaniel Hawthorne's well-known novel by the same name. The house was built in 1668 and harbors a secret staircase. The house in which Hawthorne was born has been moved to the grounds in recent years, and the complex includes two other buildings dating back to the 1600s. You can tour the complex from 9:30 a.m. to 5:30 p.m. July 1 through Labor Day and from 10:00 a.m. to 4:30 p.m. during the rest of the year. Admission is $6 for adults, $2.50 for children 6 to 17. The tour includes a short introductory film.

Salem also has many notable homes dating from the 1600s through the 1800s which are open to the public. **The Ropes Mansion,** several doors down from the Witch House on Essex Street, was built in 1727 and remodeled in 1894. It is operated by the Essex Institute. It is open June through October 10:00 a.m. to 4:00 p.m. Tuesday through Saturday, 1:00 to 4:30 p.m. Sunday. You will come across other historic homes as you walk around the town; pick up a visitor map at the Chamber of Commerce in the Town Hall at 32 Derby Square. There is a National Parks Tourist Information Office on Derby Street adjacent to Pickering Wharf, open until 6:00 p.m. in the summer. They can also provide you with information, and there is free parking behind the building. (I have had no trouble parking in the lot for several hours, but you may want to check with the park office to see if there is a time limit on the day of your visit.)

CAPE ANN

Cape Ann is not as well known as Massachusetts' southern cape, Cape Cod, yet it is closer to Boston, and its more rugged coastline typifies, to many, the traditional New England coast. From Cape Ann, you'll travel through a small corner of New Hampshire before entering Maine, or "Vacationland U.S.A." as it bills itself. Many of the heavily touristed areas in Maine are dedicated to the fine art of parting visitors from their cash; that's because many Maine natives make most of their annual income during the three summer months. Steer clear of the factory outlet meccas and enjoy the charm of quaint seacoast towns, the rocky shore, and the sweet smell of pine that permeates the air.

Suggested Schedule

8:30 a.m.	Breakfast.
9:30 a.m.	Leave Salem.
10:00 a.m.	Visit Hammond Castle Museum.
11:30 a.m.	Rockport.
1:30 p.m.	Lunch.
3:00 p.m.	Visit Plum Island and Newburyport.
5:00 p.m.	Leave for Kennebunk, Maine.
6:30 p.m.	Check in for the night.

Travel Route: Salem to Kennebunk (100 miles)
Today you'll be traveling along quite a few secondary roads that wind through small towns and at times take sudden turns, making them hard to follow. Watch route signs closely to avoid getting lost. (However, if you have the time, losing oneself on the North Shore can often be a rewarding experience.)

From Salem, take Route 1A north and cross the Beverly Bridge. From there, follow signs to Route 127 north. Driving along Route 127, you'll pass through the lovely towns of Pride's Crossing, Beverly Farms, and Manchester-by-the-Sea, where New England aristocrats hide their stately homes behind stone walls and vast lawns. Pride's Crossing railroad station has two waiting benches, one earmarked for Democrats and one for Republicans, adding a little humor to the morning commute. Often the most interesting homes and views are just off Route 127, so don't be timid. Try out a few of the more intriguing side streets.

In Manchester, you may want to wake up with an invigorating morning dip at Singing Beach, so called because the moving sand is said to sound like singing when the wind blows. (A warning to non-New Englanders: ocean water north of Boston may be a trifle colder than what you're used to.) Parking at the beach is for residents only, but the ten-minute walk from town is a pleasant one. Just be certain to park legally, for the law has no qualms about ticketing or towing your vehicle.

Continue on Route 127 north to Gloucester, stopping off at Hammond Castle on the way. At Gloucester, take 127A north to Rockport. An art colony for many years, Rockport has become somewhat commercialized recently because of its appealing seaside setting, yet the town still retains much of the charm that originally drew the artists here.

When you're ready to leave Rockport, drive through the center and follow Route 127 back to Gloucester. Four miles out of town there is a turnoff on your right to the village of Annisquam, a sleepy hamlet with beautiful oceanside homes; this route offers a quick scenic detour. Upon reaching Gloucester, take Route 128 south to Exit 14, then Route 133 north to Rowley. (Antique lovers will be pleased to know that Route 133 is lined with antique shops.) At Rowley, follow Route 1A north to Newburyport. From Newburyport, take Route 113 west to Interstate 95 north, following it to Kennebunk, Exit 3 in Maine. Interstate 95 is called the Maine Turnpike once you cross the Maine/New Hampshire state line.

The State of Maine operates an excellent tourist information center in Kittery just a few miles over the state

The North Shore

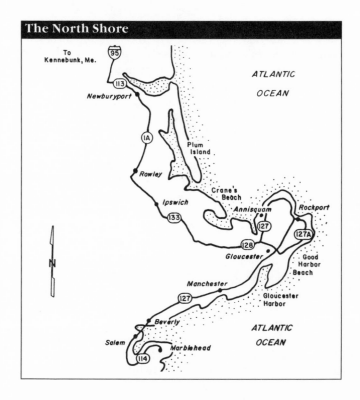

line. Accessible from the highway, it's a good place to pick up a state map ($1) and additional state tourist information from the helpful staff.

Sightseeing Highlights
▲▲The Hammond Castle Museum—The castle, at 80 Hesperus Avenue in Gloucester, was built during the late 1920s, although much of the building and its contents actually date to medieval and Renaissance Europe. The castle was built for John Hays Hammond, Jr. Though not a household name, he holds over 400 patents and is credited with many inventions that have shaped modern life, ranging from radio control systems to shaving cream. The castle interior includes an organ with over 8,000 pipes and, in the center of a medieval courtyard, a reflecting pool that Hammond used to dive into from his second-

floor bedroom window. Another unique fixture in the castle is a rain-making system, which Hammond installed in the roof over the courtyard to water his plants. On Route 127, the turnoff to Hesperus Avenue is about 4½ miles from Manchester center on your right. The street sign is not well marked from this direction, so keep your eyes peeled. Guided tours are $5 for adults, $4 for students and seniors, $3 for children 6 to 12. The castle should be open daily from 9:00 a.m. to 5:00 p.m. (last tour at 4:00 p.m.), but you may want to call ahead (508-283-2080) to verify hours during your visit, as it sometimes closes early for special events and opens late if the employees don't feel like arriving on time. The castle is closed Thanksgiving, Christmas, and New Year's Day.

▲▲ **Plum Island and Parker River National Wildlife Refuge**—This stop on the itinerary offers car-cramped legs miles of golden sand beaches to walk on and bird-watchers an opportunity to see various species in their natural habitat. The entrance fee is $5 per car, and the number of cars entering the refuge is sometimes restricted for environmental reasons. To get there, turn right onto Rolfe's Lane from Route 1A in Newbury and follow the signs. One word of caution: in early July the beaches in this area are visited by "greenheads," a type of horsefly with a nasty bite. The greenhead season only lasts about two weeks, and I've been told bug spray will repel them. Come prepared and you can still appreciate this beautiful park.

Lodging
When it comes to eating and sleeping in Kennebunk or Kennebunkport, Kennebunkport gets more tourist traffic, which means crowds and higher prices. I recommend staying in quieter Kennebunk, which is also closer to the highway. **The Kennebunk Inn** on Main Street in Kennebunk center, built in 1799, is as comfortable and charming as anything you'll find in neighboring Kennebunkport, and less costly. Double rooms range from $40 to $80 depending upon the room and the season. With the

exception of Christmas Day, the inn is open year-round. There is also an excellent restaurant on the premises. Call (207) 985-3351 for reservations.

Should you decide to join the "Bush Watchers" in Kennebunkport (President Bush's summer home is here, and tourism in the town has increased since he was inaugurated), the Federal-style **Captain Lord Mansion**, listed on the National Register of Historic Places, is a good choice. Doubles are $100 to $175 per night, including a full breakfast (207-967-3141).

As a last resort, stay at one of the two motels on opposite sides of Exit 3 in Kennebunk. They take advantage of the overflow from Kennebunkport, so their rates are just about as high, and even higher than the Kennebunk Inn's without the ambience.

Camping

Yankeeland Campground is less than 3 miles from Interstate 95. Get off I-95 north at Exit 3; a right turn at the end of the exit ramp will take you in the opposite direction from Kennebunk. Drive straight for 2.7 miles. The entrance to the campground will be on your left. Hookups, hot showers, and complete recreational facilities including swimming are all available. The campground is open from May through Columbus Day. For reservations, call (207) 985-7576.

Dining

For lunch, I recommend **Woodman's** on the causeway in Essex about 3 miles after turning onto Route 133. Woodman's is a North Shore institution serving phenomenal fried clams. Although their prices are no longer dirt cheap, portions are so large that two people should have no problem splitting a dinner. If hunger sets in before you leave Rockport, there are plenty of restaurants on Bearskin Neck or along Beach Street in the center of town.

For your evening meal in Kennebunk, **Squaretoes** on Main Street offers traditional Italian, New England, and seafood dishes at moderate prices. They also serve decent breakfasts.

The Kennebunk Inn across the street is the place to go for more refined dining. The menu changes, but New England specialties are the standard fare. Dinner entrées average about $15.

Itinerary Options

Cape Ann, with its quiet towns and excellent beaches, is a relaxing place to unwind for a few days. Crane's Beach off Route 133 in Ipswich and Good Harbor Beach off Route 127 in Gloucester are two of my favorite beaches in the area. The parking lot at Good Harbor is for residents only, but sometimes you can find parking within walking distance. For a fee, anyone can park at Crane's. On hot summer days, especially weekends, the lot fills up quickly. The Crane Mansion at nearby Castle Hill was built with money made in bathroom fixtures and is now rented out for elegant parties.

Picnics and polo go hand-in-hand at the Myopia Hunt Club. The action usually starts around 3:00 p.m. on Sunday afternoons throughout the summer and early fall. The polo grounds are off Route 1A in Hamilton. Call (508) 468-7956 for information.

Summer whale-watching expeditions are a very popular North Shore pastime. The Yankee Fleet in Gloucester operates both whale-watching cruises and deep-sea fishing trips. Call (1-800) WHALING or (508) 283-0313 for prices and schedules.

If you do stick around the North Shore for a while, Chipper's River Cafe (508-356-7956) on Market Street in Ipswich has delicious, out-of-the-ordinary sandwiches at reasonable prices. The Wenham Tea House (508-468-1398) serves simple home-cooked meals and corn muffins that will carry you back to your childhood. Wenham also has a small museum with period rooms and a doll collection. The museum is located at 132 Main Street and is open year-round Monday through Friday 9:30 a.m. to 4:30 p.m., Saturday 1:00 to 4:00 p.m., Sunday 2:00 to 5:00 p.m.

Portsmouth, New Hampshire

Although Portsmouth may not be well known outside of
New England, it is a gem of a city. In fact, even many New
Englanders aren't aware of this port city's charms, but it is
certainly worth a visit if you have time. In addition to an
extensive selection of fine shops and restaurants—most
notably, the **Blue Strawberry**, which serves fabulous
six-course dinners (29 Ceres St. overlooking the water;
reservations are a must (603-431-6420)—Portsmouth
boasts an interesting and historic waterfront district.

Strawberry Banke Museum is in the heart of the
waterfront district. The museum is really a preserved
neighborhood originally settled in the 1630s and so named
for the profusion of strawberries that once grew there
along the banks of the Piscataqua River. After existing as a
thriving community for several centuries, the area gradu-
ally deteriorated and faced demolition in the 1950s. A
group of concerned citizens stepped in and began creat-
ing the museum you see today. Forty-five buildings make
up the museum—some have been decorated with period
furnishings, some have costumed guides, some exhibit
early American tools or building methods of the day, and
a few can only be viewed from the exterior as they are
still awaiting restoration. The most interesting buildings
at Strawberry Banke include the childhood home of Victorian writer Thomas Bailey Aldrich, the beautiful Good-
win Mansion, the Dinsmore Shop where coopers make
the wooden barrels once used extensively for transporting and storing goods, and the Drisco House. The latter, a
two-family house built in 1795, is furnished on one side
in the style of the 1790s and on the other as it would have
appeared in the 1950s, an example of how a house's use
would have changed over the years. The museum is open
daily 10:00 a.m. to 5:00 p.m. May through October.
Admission is $8 for adults, $7 for seniors, $4 for children
ages 6 to 16. Admission for families with 2 or more children is $22.

In addition to Strawberry Banke, there are a number of
historic homes open to the public throughout the city.

The Moffat-Ladd House and Gardens (open Monday through Saturday 1:00 to 4:00 p.m., Sunday 2:00 to 5:00 p.m., admission $3 for adults, $.75 for children) and **The Wentworth-Gardner House** (open Tuesday through Sunday 1:00 to 4:00 p.m., admission $3) were both built around 1760. A map and guide to the historic properties is available from the Chamber of Commerce (603-436-1118). **The Portsmouth Heritage Museum** has exhibits of local history (603-431-2000).

Portsmouth also has a small **Children's Museum** located at 280 Marcy Street just a few blocks from Strawberry Banke. The museum is open Tuesday through Saturday from 10:00 a.m. to 5:00 p.m., Sunday 1:00 to 5:00 p.m., and Monday during the summer. Admission is $3.50 for both adults and children and $3 for seniors. Children under age 1 are admitted free. At Portsmouth's **Albacore Park** visitors can tour a 1952 electric and diesel submarine. The park is open daily from 9:30 a.m. to 4:30 p.m., and admission is $4 for adults, $3 for seniors, $2 for children 7 to 12, and $10 for families.

As in many New England cities, harbor and whale-watching cruises leave from the port. **Portsmouth Harbor Cruises** (603-436-8084) operates harbor cruises, and **The Isles of Shoals Steamship Company** runs excursions to the Isles and whale-watch expeditions (603-431-5500 or 1-800-441-4620). To get to Portsmouth's historic district and waterfront, take Exit 7 off Interstate 95, about 20 miles north of the center of Newburyport. You'll see signs directing you to Strawberry Banke from downtown Portsmouth.

Coastal Maine

The object of the day is to travel from Kennebunk to Bar Harbor, about a 4½-hour drive, much of it along Maine's scenic coastline. The best way to enjoy the trip is to follow the travel route at your own pace, seeing what interests you most. Whether it's browsing through Kennebunkport's shops, swimming at Kennebunk Beach in the morning, outlet shopping in Freeport, viewing fine art at the Portland Museum of Art, or picnicking on the harbor in lovely Camden, the day invites you to spend it at your leisure.

Suggested Schedule

9:00 a.m.	Leave Kennebunk.
6:00 p.m.	Arrive in Bar Harbor.

Travel Route: Kennebunk to Bar Harbor (200 miles)
Take the Maine Turnpike (Interstate 95) north from Kennebunk. If you wish to make a stop in Portland, take Interstate 295 at Exit 6A; otherwise continue on I-95 north. Although Portland is Maine's largest city, it is still small enough that any exit for downtown will take you to the center of Portland as long as you drive east. The **Old Port Exchange District** on the waterfront is being revitalized, the **Children's Museum of Maine** (open daily from 9:30 a.m. to 4:30 p.m., $2.50 per person over 1 year old) at 746 Stevens Avenue might be a mandatory stop if you're traveling with small children, and the **Portland Museum of Art** (open Tuesday through Saturday 10:00 a.m. to 5:00 p.m., Sunday from noon to 5:00 p.m., $3.50 for adults, $2.50 for seniors and students, $1 for children under 18, and free on Thursday evenings from 5:00 to 9:00 p.m.) at Congress and High streets has a wonderful collection of Winslow Homer paintings and is well respected in art circles. Interstate 295 will take you back to the turnpike if you just continue north.

The Maine Coast

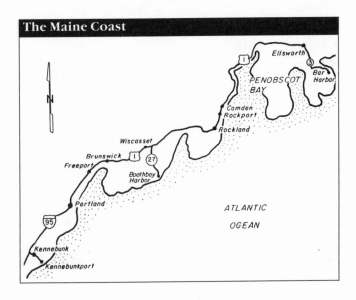

Fans of L. L. Bean and designer outlets might want to stop in the once-sleepy town of Freeport, now a mile-long strip of names like Ralph Lauren, Anne Klein, and Benetton. Good bargains can be found, and a midnight shopping spree at L. L. Bean (open 24 hours) is a rite of passage for any New England college student. To stop in Freeport, take Exit 19 off the turnpike. You can shop your way through Freeport and get right back on the highway at Exit 20 on the other end of town. If shopping is not your bag, the **Freeport Balloon Company** (207-865-1712) operates hot-air balloon rides that will take you far from the shopping mecca below.

Everyone should leave the turnpike at Exit 22 for Bath, Brunswick, and coastal Route 1. Follow Route 1 all the way up to Ellsworth, passing through the towns of Wiscasset, "the prettiest town in Maine" with a number of historic homes including the striking **Castle Tucker** overlooking Wiscasset Harbor (open Tuesday through Saturday 11:00 a.m. to 4:00 p.m. during July and August, admission is $2), Rockport (nestled in a quiet cove about a mile off Route 1), and Camden (with its harbor park overlooking Penobscot Bay). The drive from Freeport to

Camden takes a little under two hours without stops, and it is about 1½ hours more from Camden to Bar Harbor. From Rockport on, you'll catch tantalizing glimpses of the sea all along the route. Flea market buffs will find Route 1 in Searsport absolute heaven.

Those with extra time may fancy a detour onto Route 27 east and the Boothbay Peninsula, where scenic coves, quaint shops, and art galleries await visitors. There are two aquariums in the area—the **Marine Aquarium** run by the Maine Department of Marine Resources in West Boothbay Harbor (open daily Memorial Day through Labor Day with free admission) and **Oceans East Aquarium** at 87 Atlantic Avenue in Boothbay Harbor (207-633-3965). **Railway Village** on Route 27 has vintage autos, fire equipment, and trains on display (open daily 9:30 a.m. to 5:00 p.m. from mid-June through mid-October; admission $5 for adults, $2 for children).

At Ellsworth, take Route 3 east for the final 20-mile leg of the journey to Bar Harbor.

Lodging

For my money, **Daney's Cottage** (207-288-3856), on quiet, residential Hancock Street, is about the best bargain around at $10 to $18 per person. You may have to give up the luxury of a private bath, but rooms are clean and downtown Bar Harbor is only a five-minute walk. About a half block away on Main Street, **McKay's Cottages** (207-288-3531) are also reasonable. Rates including breakfast start at $47 for a double. The **Bar Harbor Inn**, in the heart of downtown right on the harbor, offers fancier accommodations. Doubles range from $95 to $195 (1-800-248-3351).

Mt. Desert Street, also convenient to downtown, has a whole string of inns. Some of the rooms at the Victorian **Mira Monte Inn** (207-288-4268) have fireplaces, and continental breakfast is included in the room rate ($75-$125). **Holbrook House** (207-288-4970) has wonderful porches, and all rooms have private baths. Rates including a full breakfast range from $90 to $110. The attractive **Primrose Cottage Inn** (207-288-4031) is a pleasant establishment, where rooms are priced from $75 to $125.

There are countless motels and cottages along Route 3 as you approach Bar Harbor from Ellsworth. If you're not planning to visit during the month of August or on a holiday weekend, you can probably check into any of these without advance reservations. The Bar Harbor Chamber of Commerce will send you free of charge a useful brochure with detailed lodging listings. Write to them at P.O. Box 158, Bar Harbor, ME 04609, or call (207) 288-5103, for your copy. If you plan to visit during the winter months, be sure to call ahead as many businesses close at the end of October.

Northeast Harbor, only 12 miles farther on Route 3 from Bar Harbor, can be a welcome alternative to Bar Harbor's summer throngs and is equally convenient to Acadia. If your budget permits, the view of the harbor from **The Asticou** (207-276-3344) is first-rate and so is the service. It is best to book well in advance, particularly for August, and the oceanside rooms naturally fill up first. Double rooms start around $200 mid-June through mid-September and cost substantially less during the off-season. In the center of Northeast Harbor, **The Maison Suisse Inn** (207-276-5223) provides attractive guest rooms complete with four-poster beds and cozy down comforters to take the nip out of the Maine night air. The inn is open seasonally from May through October. Double rooms start at $85 and suites at $145, breakfast included.

Camping
Blackwoods Campground, about 8 miles from Bar Harbor and one mile from Seal Harbor off Route 3, is the only campground in the heart of Acadia National Park. Several miles from the Seal Harbor entrance to Acadia, it is operated by the National Park Service. The sites are more heavily wooded than in most private campgrounds in the area, and there's a path to the ocean. Reservations must be made through Ticketron outlets or by mail up to

8 weeks ahead, and it is recommended that they be made at least three weeks ahead. It may be possible to obtain a site on a space-available basis upon your arrival. Generally, the earlier in the day you arrive, the better chance you'll have of success. There are bathrooms on the premises and a shower nearby. For provisions, there is a small store in Seal Harbor, and you'll find more substantial offerings at the Pine Tree Market on Main Street in Northeast Harbor about 4 miles away. Write Acadia National Park, P.O. Box 177, Bar Harbor, ME 04609, for reservations and current rate information.

There are a number of campgrounds reasonably close to Bar Harbor on Route 3 between Bar Harbor and Ellsworth. **Bar Harbor Campground** (207-288-5185) is only 4½ miles from the center of town and 3 miles from the main entrance to Acadia. Sites run from $12 to $18 per night. It has modern facilities including a heated pool. **Mount Desert Narrows Camping Resort** (207-288-4782), 8 miles from Bar Harbor, has RV hookups and ocean sites available ($12-$30 per night). **Barcadia Campground** (207-288-3520) is about 10 miles from Bar Harbor on the water. Sites range from $14 to $19.

Dining

No trip to the Maine seacoast is complete without a lobster dinner, and **Abel's Lobster Pound** on Route 198 in Mount Desert won't disappoint you. Abel's is open for dinner only. Reservations are recommended; call (207) 276-5827.

The Reading Room at the **Bar Harbor Inn** (207-288-3351) at the base of Main Street and **The Rinehart Dining Pavilion** (207-288-3358) on Eden Street in Bar Harbor both offer quality dining with arresting ocean views. While seafood dominates their menus, landlubbers will enjoy the Rinehart's Prime Rib. **George's** (207-288-4505), at 7 Stephen's Lane behind the First National Bank on Main Street, is not situated on the water, but its elegant ambience and unique presentation of traditional dishes warrant a visit. Dinner entrées start at about $15 in all three restaurants.

For more moderately priced meals, **Testa's** (207-288-3327) on Main Street has been a Bar Harbor institution for over 50 years specializing in family-style Italian cuisine and seafood dishes. Dinner entrées start around $8. **Jordan's Restaurant**, farther down Cottage Street at number 80, is *the* spot to go for breakfast. Jordan's is known for the best "blues" on the island, meaning blueberry muffins. Their blueberry pancakes are also tasty. They do a brisk business, so service is fast and curt.

Itinerary Options

There are several islands off the Maine coast that make for enjoyable summer day excursions if your schedule allows. Because of its unspoiled beauty, Monhegan has long been an artists' retreat; you can visit this small rocky island by boat. The *Balmy Days II* leaves Boothbay Harbor from Pier 8 daily at 9:30 a.m. during the summer. Call (207) 633-2284 for ticket information and reservations, and bring a good pair of walking shoes as cars are not allowed on the island.

Ferries travel to Vinalhaven and North Haven from Rockland several times a day year-round; trips take about an hour and fifteen minutes. Round-trip tickets cost about $3.50 for adults, $2 for children 5 to 12, and $15 for a car and driver. Call (207) 596-2202 for departure information. The exclusive Islesboro is only a 20-minute ferry ride from Lincolnville Beach north of Camden and may be the best island destination if your time is limited. The Blue Heron (207-734-6611) restaurant is the island's most popular dining establishment if you decide against a beach picnic. Call (207) 789-5611 for ferry ticket information.

Many find the Maine coast most captivating from the sea, making windjammer cruises a favored pastime. Maine Windjammer Cruises in Camden operate 3- and 6-day cruises with rates ranging from $275 to $545 per person. Bring lots of warm clothing if you opt for one of these scenic cruises. It can get very chilly on the water, even in midsummer.

ACADIA NATIONAL PARK

Acadia National Park is the easternmost national park in the country. If you stand atop Cadillac Mountain at dawn, they say you can be the first person in the United States to see the sunrise. The park, which encompasses rocky coastline, sheltered coves, wooded mountain trails, freshwater lakes, and ocean vistas, was donated by conservation-minded individuals to create a national park, rather than being purchased outright by the government. Today you'll see why they felt the land should be preserved.

Suggested Schedule

9:00 a.m.	Start your day in Acadia at the visitor information center, then enter the Park Loop Road.
1:00 p.m.	Picnic lunch on scenic Somme Sound.
3:30 p.m.	Enjoy tea on the lawn at the Jordan Pond Restaurant.
5:00 p.m.	Drive to Cadillac Mountain summit.
7:00 p.m.	Have a light dinner and stroll by Bar Harbor's many souvenir shops.

Travel Route
You'll drive about 50 miles before the day is over, all within the relatively small area of Mount Desert Island. Start the drive at Acadia's visitor information center, 3 miles west of Bar Harbor just off Route 3. After leaving the visitor's center, take the Park Loop Road in the direction of Sand Beach.

Visit the Wild Garden, Abbe Museum, Sand Beach, and Thunder Hole, then exit the park road at Seal Harbor and drive 3 miles to Northeast Harbor on Route 3. From the center of Northeast Harbor, follow signs to Sargent Drive which will take you by some of the more exclusive residences. Just past the Tennis Club, a turnout on your left offers a view overlooking Somme Sound, the only natural

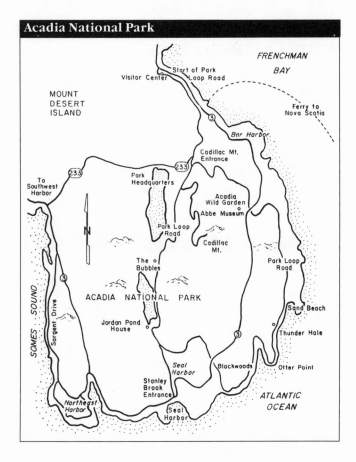

Acadia National Park

FRENCHMAN BAY

Visitor Center
Start of Park Loop Road

MOUNT DESERT ISLAND

Ferry to Nova Scotia

Bar Harbor

Cadillac Mt. Entrance

To Southwest Harbor

233

233

Park Headquarters

Acadia Wild Garden

Abbe Museum

Park Loop Road

Cadillac Mt.

The Bubbles

Park Loop Road

ACADIA NATIONAL PARK

Sand Beach

SOMES SOUND

Sargent Drive

Jordan Pond House

Thunder Hole

Seal Harbor

Blackwoods

Otter Point

Stanley Brook Entrance

Northeast Harbor

Seal Harbor

ATLANTIC OCEAN

fiord on the east coast. The spot is ideal for a picnic; just be sure to save room for afternoon tea.

If you're traveling by camper, motorcycle, or recreational vehicle, you'll need to retrace your steps at this point to the Stanley Brook entrance to Acadia (where you exited for Seal and Northeast harbors) as only automobiles are allowed on Sargent Drive and traveling it on foot is impractical. By car, follow Sargent Drive along majestic Somme Sound until it intersects with Route 3. Take Route 3 back to Northeast Harbor, reenter Park Loop Road at the Stanley Brook entrance, drive to Jordan Pond, perhaps stopping for tea, then continue on the park road to the turnoff for Cadillac Mountain. After visiting the summit, return to the Park Loop Road, then exit onto Route 233 to return to Bar Harbor.

Sightseeing Highlights
▲▲▲**Acadia National Park**—This park covers over 35,000 acres. The largest portion of the park, and the most heavily touristed, is on Mount Desert Island, so named for its treeless top by French explorer Samuel de Champlain in the early 1600s. Frenchman's Bay, whose name also derives from the French Colonial era, lies between Mount Desert Island and the Schoodic Peninsula, where there is an extension of Acadia. Entrance to the park is $5 per car for a seven-day pass. Be sure to bring your binoculars as seals and otters can often be seen playing on rocks just offshore.

The visitor information center is a good place to familiarize yourself with the park. A fifteen-minute introductory film to Acadia is shown every half hour. Pick up a free map while you are here, and a list of hiking trails if you wish to stray from the main road.

The **Wild Garden** is one of the first detours along the park loop. Plants you'll see throughout the park are labeled in this garden of wildflowers, making them easier to identify when you spot them in their natural habitat. The **Abbe Museum**, at the same turnoff, is a small museum of tools and artifacts used by the Indians who were the island's first settlers.

Back on the loop, you come to **Sand Beach**, unusual because most beaches you see on Mount Desert Island are rugged and rocky. Even on the hottest of summer days, this beach is kept cool by ocean breezes. The trail to **Great Head** starts at the far end of the beach. Farther along the park road is **Thunder Hole**, where wave erosion has created a hole in the rocks which resounds with a booming noise as the waves crash to the shore.

The restaurant at **Jordan Pond** serves a marvelous afternoon tea on the lawn with a splendid view of the pond and the "Bubbles"—two matching rounded mountains shaped by glaciers. If solitude is more your cup of tea, take a leisurely walk on the nature trail or on one of the flat paths alongside the pond. Find your own secluded rock and just soak up the scenery. The **Gate House** across the road from the restaurant is also worth a closer look because of its unique stone architecture.

The drive to **Cadillac Summit** will be the high point of your day both figuratively and literally, as it is the highest point on the Atlantic coast. Though the climb by automobile takes about ten minutes without stopping, scores of breathtaking vistas will no doubt slow your progress. (The climb and descent will put a strain on your vehicle so be sure to check the fluids and brakes before starting the ascent.) An arresting panorama awaits atop Cadillac Mountain. (Both the mountain and the luxury automobile were named after the same Frenchman.) From the summit one can see the harbors below, the Porcupine and Cranberry islands dotting the foreground, and Winter Harbor, Ironbound, and Schoodic across Frenchman's Bay. The view is particularly spectacular at sunrise or sunset, and the summit is also a popular stargazing post. The road is closed from midnight until one hour before sunrise.

Helpful Hints

Many people choose to see Acadia from a bicycle rather than through a windshield. Except for the road to Cadillac Summit, which is demanding enough for a four-cylinder engine, two-wheel transportation is a refreshing way to explore the park. Bicycles and mountain bikes can be rented in Bar Harbor from **Acadia Bike & Canoe** at 48 Cottage Street (207-288-5483) for about $15 to $20 per day.

A sightseeing cruise on Frenchman's Bay is another agreeable way to survey the park and islands. **Frenchman's Bay Boating Company** next to the municipal pier in Bar Harbor offers a variety of cruising options. Call (207) 288-3322 for more information.

Just for Kids

About 12 miles west of Bar Harbor on Route 3, a 3-mile stretch of highway has enough mini-golf courses, ice cream parlors, paddle boats, go-cart tracks, water slide parks, and even a small zoo to bring just about any travel-weary child out of the doldrums.

Itinerary Options

Those with more time may wish to go on to Southwest and Bass harbors and the western part of Acadia from Northeast Harbor, rather than return to the main Park Loop Road immediately. From Bass Harbor you can take a ferry to Swan's Island, and another ferry operates from Northeast Harbor to the Cranberry Islands. There are also over 120 miles of trails within Acadia to tempt the hiker. If you are so inclined and have the opportunity to stay a day or two longer, investigate some of them on your own.

Schoodic Peninsula, directly across Frenchman's Bay from Bar Harbor, is also part of Acadia National Park. Because of its distance from the heart of Acadia, Schoodic is much less traveled but no less scenic. Take an extra day to traverse this more remote part of the park and the quiet fishing village of Winter Harbor. To get there, you'll need to take Route 3 back to Ellsworth and continue on US 1 north to West Gouldsboro. From there take Route 186 to Winter Harbor.

For those with lots of time on their hands, Nova Scotia is just a 6-hour ferry ride from Bar Harbor on the *Blue-nose.* From mid-June through mid-September, the famous ferry departs daily for Yarmouth at 8:00 a.m. One-way passenger fare is $36.25 for adults, $18.15 for children 5 to 12. Automobiles and mobile homes up to 20 feet cost $67 one-way. The ferry runs on a reduced schedule the rest of the year, and fares are lower. Call (1-800) 432-7344 or (207) 288-3397 for further information and reservations. Gambling is allowed on board once the ship reaches international waters. In Nova Scotia, the most scenic routes are along the coasts. The Cabot Trail on Cape Breton at the easternmost end of Nova Scotia is generally considered to be the province's most beautiful region. From Caribou, Nova Scotia, you can take the ferry to sleepy Prince Edward Island where deserted white sand beaches meet a surprisingly warm, blue sea.

MT. WASHINGTON

The trip across Maine, approximately four hours from Bar Harbor to Bethel, is the longest stretch of straight driving without a stop on the entire trip. However, as you approach the White Mountains, the views make the journey quite a pleasant one. The beauty of western Maine and New Hampshire's White Mountain National Forest is today's focal point.

Suggested Schedule

7:30 a.m.	Early breakfast at Jordan's.
8:30 a.m.	Leave Bar Harbor.
12:30 p.m.	Lunch in Bethel, Maine.
2:30 p.m.	Take the auto road to the top of Mt. Washington, the highest peak in the northeastern United States.
6:00 p.m.	Check into your accommodations.
7:00 p.m.	Dine in either Jackson or North Conway.

Travel Route: Bar Harbor to Mt. Washington (200 miles)

Take Route 3 west from Bar Harbor to Ellsworth. At Ellsworth, follow US 1A toward Bangor. Just before Bangor, take Interstate 395 west, to US 2, which will take you all the way to Gorham, New Hampshire. In the center of Gorham, turn left onto Route 16 south. The entrance to the Mt. Washington Auto Road is about 8 miles from Gorham on your right. After a stop at Mt. Washington, take Route 16 to Jackson or continue to North Conway.

Sightseeing information is not the only reason to stop at the information center on Route 16 in Intervale just outside North Conway. The panorama of the Mt. Washington Valley from the parking lot is one of the finest around.

Sightseeing Highlights

▲▲▲**Mt. Washington**—At 6,288 feet, this is the highest peak in the Northeast, and on clear days, the panoramas from the ascent and summit are unrivaled. On top are a weather station and complete tourist facilities. Even in July the peak's climate can be quite brisk, so be sure to bring warm clothing with you. The summit can be reached by the auto road in your own vehicle at a cost of $12 for car and driver, plus $5 each additional adult, $3 for children 5 to 12. The auto road is open from mid-May to mid-October, weather permitting. However, you should not take those bumper stickers that read "This Car Climbed Mt. Washington" lightly; the climb to the top is not easy, even for an automobile in top-notch condition. Should you prefer not to put the wear and tear on your car, vans are available to take riders up the mountain: $16 for adults, $10 for children 5 to 12. After five hours on the road, you may find it a welcome relief to let a tour guide do the driving. There is also cog-railway service available from the other side of Mt. Washington at Bretton Woods. The round-trip by rail costs $32 for adults and takes three hours.

Of course, many hikers try their luck at climbing the mountain. Should you wish to do so, you'll need a whole day. The information center across from the entrance to the auto road can suggest trails that are right for your ability. It is fairly easy for weary hikers to get rides back down the mountain from people who have taken the auto road. Camping shelters along the trail provide sanctuary for hikers who get caught in bad weather or who just want to spend more time exploring the region.

▲**Gondola Skyride**—For a different perspective of Mt. Washington, take the gondola at Wildcat Ski Area, which faces the mountain. The ride operates daily during July, August, and September from 10:00 a.m. to 4:30 p.m. and on weekends only during June. Tickets are $6.50 for adults, $3 for children 6 to 12.

Jackson

About 8 miles south of Wildcat is a covered bridge leading to the town of Jackson. Although Jackson does have
Black Mountain downhill ski area, the town is best known
as a cross-country skiers' haven, so there are plenty of
cozy bed and breakfasts around to take care of tired winter and summer visitors alike.

North Conway

Mt. Cranmore in nearby North Conway is one of the
oldest ski areas in the Northeast. Although rail service is
no longer available, trains used to arrive from Boston on a
regular basis, dropping skiers off right in the heart of the
village. For this reason, the town has been catering to
tourists for many years and the effects are beginning to
show. In the past ten years, factory outlets and the multi-
tude of shoppers they bring have begun to crowd the
town's charming core. Still, North Conway has its appeal,
which includes the greatest variety of shops, restaurants,
and lodging establishments in the Mt. Washington valley.

▲**Cathedral Ledge**—Just a few minutes from the center
of North Conway, the ledge draws throngs of rock climbers
and spectators alike. You'll probably find this daring sport
fascinating to watch if you've never witnessed it firsthand. Climbers can be observed from below, or you can
drive up the road to the top of the ledge and congratulate
the climbers as they reach their goal. Cool off after watching the climbers with a swim at neighboring **Echo Lake
State Park**.

▲**The Conway Scenic Railroad**—The railroad runs
out of North Conway's picturesque depot, which was
built in 1874, travels south along the Saco River, crosses
the Swift River to the town of Conway, and is enjoyable to
young and old alike. Tickets for the one-hour excursion
are $7 for adults, $4.50 for children 4 to 12. First-class
tickets in the "Gertrude Emma," a 92-year-old restored
parlor car, cost an additional $3. Departure times are
11:00 a.m. and 1:00, 2:30, and 4:00 p.m. daily from the
second Saturday in June through the fourth Sunday in

October, on Thanksgiving weekend, and the three
weekends before Christmas. In July and August there is
also the Sunset Special, which leaves on Tuesday,
Wednesday, Thursday, and Saturday nights at 7:00 p.m.
Call (603) 356-5251 for information.

Mt. Washington Valley
There is plenty for children to do in the valley. **Storyland**
on Route 16 in Glen, a favorite of youngsters, is open
daily from Father's Day to Labor Day and on weekends
only Labor Day through Columbus Day (603-383-4293).
Four miles west of the junction of US 302 and Route 16,
Attitash Ski Area in Bartlett operates an alpine slide and
water park during the summer. There is a mountain
stream swimming hole at Jackson. Just follow the signs
from Jackson center toward the Eagle Mountain House.
The swimming hole is about halfway up the hill on your
right.

Lodging
The Eagle Mountain House in Jackson is a charming
resort on a quiet country road with beautiful mountain
views. The rooms in the recently restored hotel are com-
fortably elegant and a relative bargain, starting at $100
during the height of fall foliage season and $60 during
early spring and late fall. Suites start at $115 during the
summer and $90 in off-season. Tennis, golf, and swim-
ming are all available at the resort as well. Follow signs up
Carter Notch Road from the center of Jackson. Call
(1-800) 527-5022 or (603) 383-9111 for reservations.

   The Inn at Thorn Hill, in a home designed by
renowned architect Stanford White, is another lovely
lodging option in Jackson village. Rooms are tastefully
decorated with Victorian furnishings, and rates starting at
$55 per person include lodging, a hearty breakfast, and
gourmet evening meal (603-383-4242).

   The Cranmore Inn, only one block from the center
of North Conway on Kearsarge Street, is more reasonably
priced than many other inns in town yet offers the same

services. A comfortable room for two costs from $35 to
$85 per night (depending on the season) including an
ample breakfast in the inn's sunny breakfast room. There
are several sitting rooms and a swimming pool on the
premises. Mt. Cranmore ski area is only five minutes away.
Call (603) 356-5502 or (1-800) 822-5502 for reservations.

Route 16 in North Conway is lined with inns and motels,
which can fill up at the height of fall foliage or for big ski
weekends. If you're calling ahead, try **The Scottish Lion**
(603-356-6381). The rooms are pleasant, meals have a
Scottish slant, and there is a lively pub to unwind in after
a long day of sightseeing or skiing. Rooms including a full
breakfast range from $50 to $70. The inn also operates a
Scottish import shop next door. **The White Trellis
Motel**, with pleasant mountain views, makes more of an
effort than most to create an attractive atmosphere with
flowering window boxes and ivy covered trellises. Doubles range from $38 to $65 depending on the season
(603-356-2492). **The Hearths & Hillsides Bed and
Breakfast Association** can also help you book a room
in the area (603-356-9460 or 1-800-562-1300).

Camping

Dolly Copp Campground is a national forest campground with 176 sites near the base of Mt. Washington off
Route 16, 6 miles south of Gorham. Reservations can be
made by the MISTIX reservation system (1-800-283-CAMP).
If you arrive without a reservation, sites are assigned on a
first-come, first-served basis. RVs are allowed, but hot
showers and electrical hookups are not available. Sites
average about $8 per night. The campground is open from
mid-May to mid-October.

Glen Ellis Family Campground, on US 302 just west
of the Route 16 junction, is convenient to Jackson, North
Conway, and tomorrow's travel route. In case you are
low on provisions, there is a supermarket located next to
the entrance. The campground itself has complete sani-
tary and recreational facilities. Some sites are adjacent to

the Saco River. The campground operates seasonally from Memorial Day to Columbus Day, July being the busiest month. Call (603) 383-9320 for information in season or (516) 746-2759 for inquiries during the winter.

Dining

The Millbrook Tavern at the Bethel Inn in Bethel, Maine, is a good place to stop for lunch. The inn is open year-round, and outdoor dining on the terrace is available during the summer months. Lunch prices start at $5 for sandwiches. Those with extra time, and golf clubs or tennis rackets, might choose to make use of the inn's sports facilities. The inn is also an agreeable home base should you wish to linger in the area. If you are traveling with your own provisions, there are plenty of picnic areas along US 2 that can accommodate an alfresco meal nicely.

For dinner, there is fine dining in Jackson at **The Eagle Mountain House**. More moderately priced meals can be had at the **Thompson House Eatery** right in the center of Jackson (603-383-9341). Not too far from Jackson, **The Bernerhof Inn** on US 302 west in Glen, just 2 miles from the Route 16 intersection, serves appetizing European dishes with a German flair (603-383-4414).

In North Conway just across from the railroad depot on Main Street, **Horsefeathers'** menu ranges from deluxe burgers to pasta and chicken entrées. The tavern atmosphere is lively, and prices are moderate at $4.95 to $12.95 (603-356-2687). Also in North Conway's center on Seavey Street one block up from Main Street, **Bellini's** serves Italian specialties including homemade pastas prepared in delicious combinations. Try the fettucini with prosciutto, spinach, and mushrooms in a light cream sauce. If you have room, their desserts are also scrumptious. Dinner entrées range from $7.95 to $16.95 (603-356-7000). For reasonably priced blueberry pancake and omelet breakfasts, try the **Big Pickle Restaurant** next door to Bellini's on Seavey Street.

The Arts
The Eastern Slope Playhouse next door to the Eastern Slope Inn on Main Street in North Conway presents professional musical productions during the summer months. Call (603) 447-2177 for schedule and ticket information.

Itinerary Options
The Oxford Hills region of Maine near Bethel, with beautiful freshwater Lakes Norway, Thompson, and Long, a mineral- and gem-rich landscape, and numerous wooded trails, is a pleasant place for hikers, rock-hounds, and fishermen to spend some extra time.

More adventurous travelers may find a river trip to their liking. **Saco Bound** in Conway, New Hampshire, operates a variety of river trips including whitewater and flatwater, by raft or canoe, for several hours, or several days. Contact them at (603) 447-2177 or Box 119, Center Conway, NH 03813, for more details.

WHITE MOUNTAIN NATIONAL FOREST

The White Mountain National Forest is a 750,000-acre expanse in central New Hampshire which encompasses much of the Presidential Range, including 6,288-foot Mt. Washington, as well as a bounty of alpine lakes, streams, cascades, and hiking trails. Today you'll explore this lush region before crossing the border into Vermont.

Suggested Schedule

8:00 a.m.	Breakfast.
9:00 a.m.	Spend the morning and early afternoon savoring the White Mountain National Forest's natural attractions. Enjoy a picnic lunch with an alpine backdrop.
2:00 p.m.	Leave the national forest and travel to Woodstock, Vermont, pausing along the way to visit a mine, a maple sugarhouse, a glassblowing exhibit, or an early farm museum, or hike to the bottom of a gorge.
6:00 p.m.	Check into your lodging.
7:00 p.m.	Dinner.

Travel Route: Jackson/North Conway to Woodstock, Vermont (150 miles)

Route 16 south from Jackson or north from North Conway intersects with US 302 at Glen. Take US 302 west toward Bartlett and Twin Mountain. You will be passing through Crawford Notch State Park. At Twin Mountain, take US 3 south until it merges with Franconia Notch Parkway. Continue south on the parkway, exiting to see the forest's natural attractions. Exits are marked, and parking is provided.

Leaving Franconia Notch State Park, stay on US 3 south to Interstate 93 south. The mountain views from I-93 are breathtaking. Exit I-93 at Route 104 west. At Danbury, proceed on US 4 west all the way to Woodstock, Vermont.

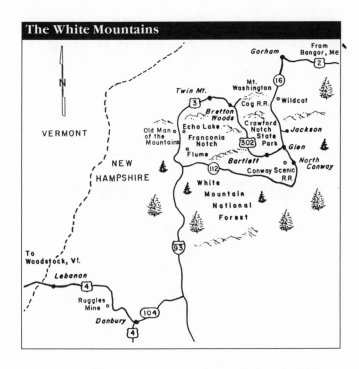

The White Mountains

Alternate Route: From Lincoln just below the Flume, take Route 112 west to Route 118 south. At Warren, Route 118 merges with Route 25. Continue south to Wentworth, then follow Route 25A west to Fairlee, and from there take Route 10 south to Hanover, home of **Dartmouth College**, the Ivy League's northernmost member. **The Hood Museum of Art** at Dartmouth has European, Asian, and American pieces, as well as works by twentieth-century artists including Picasso, and the **Baker Memorial Library** has Orozco frescoes.

After visiting Hanover, cross the Connecticut River to Norwich, Vermont. From Norwich, follow US 5 south to White River Junction where you can pick up US 4 west to Woodstock. This alternate route enables you to see the lovely college town of Hanover but will not save you any time over the main travel route.

Crawford Notch State Park is in the heart of the White Mountain National Forest. As you travel through the park, you'll pass two small waterfalls, the Silver and Flume cascades, that slither rather than plunge down the mountainside. Both have parking areas. The better mountain view is from the Flume Cascade parking lot. The park's information center is located in a colorful train station near Twin Mountain.

As you near Twin Mountain, there is a striking view of the Mt. Washington Hotel at Bretton Woods. Built in 1902, the hotel was designed to entice the privileged set, and it still holds a commanding presence over the valley. In its heyday, visitors came by the trainload to visit the hotel. Today Bretton Woods is a thriving cross-country ski mecca. The entrance to the **Cog Railway** that climbs Mt. Washington is just beyond the hotel. The three-hour round-trip to the summit costs $32 for adults, $30 for seniors, $20 for children 7 to 15, children under 6 free. The train runs from May to November 1. The railway recommends advance ticket purchase. Call (1-800) 922-8825, ext. 7, or (603) 846-5404, ext. 7, for reservations.

Cannon Mountain Ski Area is at the northern entrance to **Franconia Notch State Park**. Cannon operates a tramway during nonskiing months ($7 for adults, $3.50 for children 6 to 12; combination tickets to the tram and the Flume are $10 for adults, $5 for children). While at Cannon, you can also visit the **New England Ski Museum** to learn more about the regional history of the sport through an audiovisual presentation. The museum is open from mid-May through mid-October, and again just after Christmas for the winter ski season, from noon to 5:00 p.m., closed on Wednesday. Admission $1 for adults, and free for children.

The turnoff to **Old Man of the Mountain** is just after Cannon Mountain and **Echo Lake.** This portion of cliffs overlooking **Profile Lake** was so named because erosion has given the granite the appearance of an old man from certain angles. Nathaniel Hawthorne wrote about the famous formation in his short story, "The Great Stone Face." You will see the old man's profile on many of New Hampshire's highway route signs.

Other highlights of the park include **the Basin** and
the Flume. Swirling with water, the Basin is a natural
pothole formed by ice age glaciers and mountain cascades. There is wheelchair access, and swimming is pro-
hibited. A well-maintained bike path runs through this
section of the park, and hiking trails abound. You may
wish to hike one of the trails that leave from the Basin
area, which are free and likely to be less crowded than
the Flume trail.

The Flume is a narrow, moss-covered granite gorge dis-
covered in 1808 by Jesse Guernsey, a 93-year-old woman
who was hoping to find a prime fishing spot. After hiking
the Flume, you can return to the visitors center or continue on the trail to view a waterfall and natural pool.
Plan to spend about an hour and a half here if you decide
to hike the entire loop. Although there are buses that can
take you from the visitors center halfway to the Flume,
much of the arduous walking still lies ahead, and there is
no handicapped access. The trail is refreshingly cool on
hot summer days, but on brisk autumn days you may
want to bring an extra sweater or jacket along. The Flume
is open from 9:00 a.m. to 4:30 p.m. daily, June through
October. There is a separate admission charge of $5 for
adults, $2.50 for children 6 to 12, if you decided not to
purchase combination tickets at the Cannon Mountain
tram.

In contrast to the park's natural attractions, there is a
small amusement park, Fantasy Farm, a waterslide park,
and the Whale's Tail, on US 3 just below the Flume.

Rock collectors may want to stop at **Ruggles Mine**
near Grafton off US 4 between Interstate 93 and White
River Junction. The mine first opened in 1803 and is
known for its vast supply of mica. Visitors are allowed to
take home mineral samples that they collect, probably
accounting for the mine's steep admission charge ($9 for
adults, $3 for children 4 to 11). The mine is open on
weekends only from mid-May through mid-June, daily
mid-June through mid-October 9:00 a.m. to 5:00 p.m.

Just after you pass into Quechee, Vermont, on US 4,
only a few miles from the Vermont/New Hampshire state

line, there is an information booth on your left. Several hundred yards beyond that, a bridge crosses the dramatic **Quechee Gorge**, 165 feet deep. Parking is available on both sides of the bridge. Take the one-mile hike to the bottom of the gorge, or just stretch your legs on the short (one-quarter mile) hike to view the waterfall that empties into the river below. There are picnic tables adjacent to the gorge.

A right-hand turn at the first blinking light after the gorge bridge will take you through one of New England's rustic covered bridges and into "downtown" Quechee. There, Simon Pearce has completely renovated the old mill so today you can watch glassblowers and potters at their crafts. You can also inspect the modern hydraulic power system that now fuels the ovens. The handmade glassware and pottery is sold in the gift shop along with natural fiber fabrics. The shop is open from 10:00 a.m. to 5:00 p.m. and you can watch glassblowing during those same hours, except from 1:00 to 2:00 p.m. when the craftsmen take their lunch. Admission is free. There is a fine restaurant on the premises as well.

From Simon Pearce, continue on River Road for several miles past lush green golf courses and farms. Should you wish to visit a maple sugarhouse to learn about processing the sweet syrup, turn onto Hillside Road and follow signs to Sugarbush Farm. Although sugaring season is in the spring, the farm is open year-round and also makes tasty Vermont cheeses. Call (802) 457-1757 for hours of operation during your visit. Should you visit Sugarbush Farm, return to River Road and cross the Taftsville Covered Bridge, which will take you back onto US 4. Woodstock is only 3 miles west.

Woodstock appears to be the type of town that crime or hardship never touches, a model New England town with elegant Federal-style homes surrounding the Town Green where every blade of grass seems perfectly groomed. Some of the bells in Woodstock's churches were made by Paul Revere himself. A tourist information booth right on the Green will provide answers to questions. The booth is open from 10:00 a.m. to 6:00 p.m.

The Town Crier Chalk Board in the center of the business district lists the goings-on for the day.

The Billings Farm & Museum is off Route 12 north of Woodstock. The farm offers a look at rural Vermont life of a century ago. You can help hand-churn butter, see how cows were milked the old-fashioned way, and watch woodcarving demonstrations. The farm is open daily from late May through late October from 10:00 a.m. to 5:00 p.m. Admission is $5 for adults, $2 for children.

The Woodstock Historical Society operates the **Dana House Museum** at 26 Elm Street. Woodstock artifacts, period furnishings, antique costumes, tools, and toys make up the majority of the exhibits. The museum is open May through October, Monday through Saturday 10:00 a.m. to 5:00 p.m., Sunday 2:00 p.m. to 5:00 p.m, and weekends during December.

Woodstock also boasts an unusual museum—**The Vermont Raptor Center** at Vermont's Institute of Natural Science on Church Hill Road about 1½ miles from the Green. At the outdoor museum visitors can view over 25 species of New England hawks, owls, and eagles, including bald eagles and the great horned owl. All the birds are injured so that they cannot be released into the wild, but here the birds are protected and can be studied by those of us who might never have the opportunity to see them in their natural habitat. The center is open from 10:00 a.m. to 4:00 p.m., closed on Tuesday May through October, and closed both Tuesday and Sunday November through April. Admission is $3.50 for adults, $1 for children 5 to 11.

Lodging

For those looking for the comfort of a country inn combined with resort amenities such as golf, tennis, and swimming, **The Woodstock Inn & Resort** right on the Green is the place to stay. Double rooms start at $120 per night. Call (802) 457-1100 or (1-800) 448-7900 for reservations.

The Lincoln Covered Bridge Inn on US 4 in nearby West Woodstock is a 200-year-old farmhouse overlooking the Lincoln Covered Bridge and the Ottauquechee River. Double room rates including a full country breakfast run from $96 to $125. There is also a restaurant on the premises. Call (802) 457-3312 for reservations. **The Kedron Valley Inn** on Route 106 in South Woodstock is known for its French cuisine and has accommodations with canopy beds and country patchwork quilts. Rooms range from $98 to $169 including breakfast. The **Braeside Motel** on the east side of Woodstock offers accommodations at moderate prices (802-457-1366), and Rutland, about 40 minutes farther along US 4 west, has a much wider selection of reasonably priced lodging establishments.

Camping
The closest camping area to Woodstock is the state-operated **Quechee Recreation Area** near the Quechee Gorge. A trail runs from the camping area to the bottom of the gorge. Both tent and camper sites are available. For information, call (802) 295-2990.

Dining
Bentley's Restaurant, in Woodstock center (802-457-3232), serves dishes ranging from veal to Szechuan to fresh salads. Dinner entrées are priced from $12.95 to $17.50. Families may want to try **Spooner's Restaurant** in Spooner Barn on US 4 just east of Woodstock center. Spooner's has a children's menu, and specialties include western-style beef and traditional New England fare (802-457-4022). Prices are moderate ($7.95-$17.95).

For elegant dining, **The Prince and the Pauper** on Elm Street in Woodstock might even please royalty. The prix fixe menu ($28 per person) changes weekly, but dishes such as poached salmon and roast duckling are the norm. Call (802) 457-1818 for reservations.

Itinerary Options
For those with extra time, Day 10 is an excellent place for jumping off the itinerary to explore the Lakes Region of

New Hampshire or to spend several days in northern Vermont, before continuing on to southern Vermont and the
Berkshires.

The Lakes Region

To visit New Hampshire's largest lakes, Squam and Winnipesaukee, continue south on Route 3, then east on
Route 104 after traveling through Franconia Notch State
Park. Weirs Beach is perhaps the most touristed spot on
Winnipesaukee, complete with a honky-tonk boardwalk
and the type of sandy beach normally found at seaside
resorts. Despite its touristy nature, Weirs Beach does have
beautiful views of the lake, and many excursion companies leave from there. **Winnipesaukee Flagship**
operates three-hour boat cruises late May through late
October and Moonlight Dinner/Dance Cruises at night at
the height of the summer season. Day cruises cost about
$12 for adults, $6 for children. Moonlight dinner cruises
are $25 per person. Call (603) 366-5531 for departure
times and tickets.

The **Winnipesaukee Railroad** runs lakeside scenic
railroad trips in restored historic railroad cars. Excursions
leave from Weirs Beach and Meredith. One-hour trips are
$6 for adults, $3 for children, and two-hour trips are $7
for adults, $4 for children. The railroad operates on week-
ends only from Memorial Day through late June, then
daily through mid-October. Call (603) 279-3196 for information.

Other Lakes Region attractions include **Annalee's
Doll Museum** in Meredith, **Castle in the Clouds** in
Moultonboro, the **Polar Caves** in Plymouth, and the
water slide and surf coaster at Weirs Beach. There are
numerous accommodations and restaurants along Route
3 throughout the region.

Northern Vermont

Almost more than any other northeastern state, Vermont
embodies the spirit of New England many travelers hope
to discover when they visit this part of the world. Picture-

perfect town greens, winding river valleys, and the beautiful Green Mountains that turn gentle shades of pastel colors at sunset, all seem virtually unspoiled by modern development. If you have extra time and wish to explore this area more thoroughly, I suggest the following addition to your itinerary.

From the North Conway/Jackson area travel south on Route 16 to Conway. At Conway, take the scenic Kancamagus Highway (Route 112) west to Interstate 93 north in Lincoln. I-93 will take you through Franconia Notch State Park, and you can visit the same sites (the Flume, the Old Man of the Mountains, the Ski Museum, etc.) as described in the main itinerary for Day 10, only you will come upon them in the opposite order.

Continue on I-93 north to St. Johnsbury, Vermont, then take US 2 west. Maple syrup lovers may want to visit the **Maple Grove Museum and Factory** on US 2 in St. Johnsbury. The museum is really just a small cottage where sugaring tools are displayed and a flat vat of syrup boils. Of more interest is the video on maple syrup making that plays continuously in the gift shop and the tour of the factory where maple candy is made. Visitors can tour the factory on weekdays year-round every 12 minutes from 8:00 a.m. to 11:45 a.m. and 12:30 p.m. to 4:15 p.m. for $.50.

From St. Johnsbury, travel on US 2 west only briefly, then take Route 15 west to Jeffersonville. At Jeffersonville, take Route 108 south through Smugglers Notch, past Mt. Mansfield and the Stowe ski area to the town of Stowe. At one point the road becomes very steep, narrow, and curvy but only for a short stretch. Alongside the road there are picnic areas and entrances to hiking trails.

Restaurants and accommodations are plentiful in Stowe—long a summer and winter resort—making it a good stopping place for the night. Perhaps the best-known hotel in Stowe is the **Trapp Family Lodge**, run by the Trapp family of "The Sound of Music" fame. With its chalet-style buildings bursting with flower boxes, and unrivaled views of Stowe below and the mountains beyond, the lodge easily lives up to its motto "a little of Austria . . . a lot of Vermont." During the summer there are outdoor evening concerts in the Trapp Family Meadow. Doubles range from $125 to $255. The **Green Mountain Inn**, right in the heart of the village, is more centrally located and more affordably priced. Doubles cost $69 to $130. (802-253-7301 or 1-800-445-6629.) There is an excellent reservation service (1-800-24-STOWE) that can help book a room for you in your price range. In addition to some of the best skiing and hiking in New England, Stowe has good shopping, in-town recreational trails, an alpine slide at the mountain, and an auto toll road up Mt. Mansfield with outstanding views.

The next day head to Burlington (Vermont's largest city, although a small city by comparison to most) and Shelburne via Waterbury. Leaving Stowe take Route 100 south, which passes **Cold Hollow Cider Mill** and **Ben & Jerry's Ice Cream Factory**, both of which operate plant tours. Actually, there isn't much to see at Cold Hollow—the cider press and jelly kitchen aren't exactly exciting—but the cider samples are tasty, as are the other Vermont-made gourmet foods available for sampling and purchase. The Ben & Jerry's factory tour is fun for the whole family. Half of the $1 tour fee goes to charity, and the delectable ice cream samples fresh off the production line are well worth the other $.50.

From Waterbury take US 89 northwest to Burlington. On the shores of Lake Champlain, it is home to the University of Vermont. Ferry rides across the lake to New York state are a pleasant way to see the lake and the Adirondack and Green mountains that surround it, but keep in mind you'll need to save at least a full afternoon or morning to visit the Shelburne Museum south of Burlington. Ferries operate from Burlington late May through late October, and the crossing takes 1 hour each way. Round-trip for a car and driver costs $20, and there is a maximum charge of $25 per car. Call (802) 864-9804 for departure times during your visit. (If you really want to extend your trip, Montreal, Canada, is only about two hours north of Burlington.)

From Burlington travel on US 7 south to the **Shelburne Museum**, generally considered to have one of the best collections of early American antiques and folk art. The museum covers 45 acres and has 37 period homes housing its collection of art, china, silver, scrimshaw, Native American artifacts, carousel animals, decoys, weathervanes, ship figureheads, and antique toys and dolls. Some of the unique structures include a lighthouse, a round barn, a sidewheeler boat called the SS *Ticonderoga*, and a private railroad car. Built in the late 1800s, the latter has a plush interior of mahogany paneling, velvet upholstery, and modern bath and kitchen facilities.

Not to be missed is the hat and fragrance house, which contains much more than its name implies. Within its walls you'll find an especially fine assemblage of antique quilts, handwoven rugs, handmade lace, embroidered samplers, and costumes. The old-time country store, apothecary shop, and doctor's and dentist's offices in the general store building are fascinating; and the Electra Havemeyer Webb Memorial Building (built in memory of the woman philanthropist who founded the museum) has Degas, Manet, Rembrandt, and Monet originals. The museum is open from 9:00 a.m. to 5:00 p.m. daily from mid-May to mid-October. Admission (which will let you into the museum for two consecutive days) is $12.50 for adults, $4.50 for children 6 to 17.

After visiting the museum, you may wish to see nearby **Shelburne House and Farms** owned by Electra Havemeyer Webb's family. The estate, built in 1899, is stunningly set on Lake Champlain. Park architect Frederick Law Olmstead was consulted in the landscape design of the property. The estate now serves as an elegant inn open from late May through mid-October. Doubles range from $100 to $230 (802-985-8498 or 802-985-8686). Visitors can tour the farm daily beginning at 9:30 a.m., with the last tour leaving at 3:30 p.m., late May through mid-October. The farm makes its own delicious cheddar cheese that can be purchased at the farm store and visitor center. Proceeds go to the farm's nonprofit conservation education organization.

In addition to the Inn at Shelburne Farms, there are numerous motels along US 7 between Shelburne and Burlington. If you have time to travel one hour south to Middlebury, I recommend staying there for the night, as it will put you in better range for rejoining the main itinerary. Middlebury is a pleasant college town bisected by Otter Creek Falls. **The Middlebury Inn** is the popular place in town to stay (802-388-4961 or 1-800-842-4666), and the **Otter Creek Bakery** at 1 College Street has terrific breakfast pastries, bread sticks, and picnic fixings.

From Middlebury, continue about one hour south on US 7 to Rutland. Follow the schedule for Day 11 from there, beginning with a visit to Wilson Castle or the Vermont Marble exhibit, then again south on US 7 to Manchester.

Southern Vermont

This area of New England is particularly well traveled in autumn because of the abundant maple trees that turn brilliant orange and red as winter approaches. Southern Vermont's excellent ski resorts, beautiful mountain vistas, and charming towns with their tidy village greens are reason enough to visit the region in any season.

Suggested Schedule

8:00 a.m.	Have breakfast, then leave Woodstock for Manchester. Visit the Marble Exhibit or Wilson Castle in Proctor on the way.
11:30 a.m.	Window-shop in Manchester Center and stroll along lovely Manchester Village's marble sidewalks.
1:00 p.m.	Lunch.
2:00 p.m.	Visit Hildene.
4:00 p.m.	Take the Sky Line Drive to the top of Mt. Equinox, or if the weather refuses to cooperate, take your pick of the area's many other attractions.
6:00 p.m.	Check into a country inn for a memorable evening of fine dining and provincial comfort.

Travel Route: Woodstock to Manchester (64 miles)
From Woodstock, take US 4 to Rutland, passing by Killington and Pico ski areas, to connect with US 7. To visit either Wilson Castle or the Marble Exhibit travel on business US 4 past Rutland to West Proctor Road just past the junction with Route 3 north. Turn right onto West Proctor Road; the entrance to the castle is up about a mile on your left. The town of Proctor is five miles farther, and once there follow signs to the Marble Exhibit. After visiting these sites, backtrack to the junction of US 4 and US 7, and then take US 7 south from Rutland to Manchester Center. All along this highway there are views of the

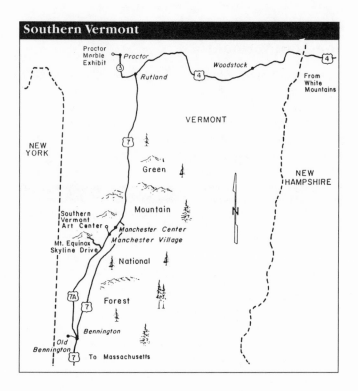

Southern Vermont

Green Mountains on your left. Historic Manchester Village is one mile from Manchester Center on Route 7A.

Manchester Center has an array of tidy shops interspersed with Ralph Lauren and Liz Claiborne outlets, among others. The Northshire Bookstore at the intersection of US 7 and Route 30 is one of the best bookstores in New England and is definitely worth a visit. Orvis, the mail order giant, has its flagship store on Route 7A in Manchester. The Equinox Valley Nursery on Route 7A is known for its colorful seasonal displays. The nursery's annual fall pumpkin patch is especially festive.

The Chamber of Commerce, located on the Green as you enter Manchester Center on US 7 traveling south, is very helpful with sightseeing information. They're open from 9:00 a.m. to 5:00 p.m. during the week, and from 10:00 a.m. to 4:00 p.m. on weekends. Hikers will want to stop in at the U.S. Forest Service office on Route 30 just east of Manchester Center. They will furnish you with local hiking suggestions. Skiers will be pleased to know that both Stratton and Bromley mountains are convenient to the Manchester area. Bromley also operates an Alpine Ride during the summer months for $4.50.

Sightseeing Highlights

▲**Vermont Marble Exhibit**—Proctor, a small town about 8 miles from Rutland, calls itself the "marble capital of the world" because of the abundance of marble found in the area. At the Vermont Marble Exhibit on Main Street visitors have the chance to see a marble sculptor at work. There is also a film explaining the natural forces that created marble and the steps man takes to mold this stone for his purposes. You will see examples of Vermont marble throughout Proctor and, later in the day, as the sidewalks of Manchester Village. The exhibit is open daily mid-May through late October from 9:00 a.m. to 5:30 p.m., and there is an admission charge. During the winter only, the gift shop is open Monday through Saturday 9:00 a.m. to 4:00 p.m.

▲▲**Wilson Castle**—On West Proctor Road off Business US 4, west of Rutland about one-half mile from the Route 3 north turnoff, the nineteenth-century castle is set on 115 acres. Built by a Vermont doctor and his wealthy British wife, the castle is filled with an eclectic mix of European and Oriental pieces. Although the paint is peeling here and there, the hand-painted and hand-stenciled ceilings are unusual, and the colorful stained and etched glass windows throughout the house are quite beautiful. A Louis XV chair used by several popes, an ornate jewel case, an inlaid pool table, and a handsome curly maple fireplace in the master bedroom are a few of the other furnishings worth special note. The castle is open daily for guided tours from late May through mid-October from 9:00 a.m. to 6:00 p.m. $6 for adults, $5.50 for seniors, $2 for children 6 to 12, children under 6 free.

▲**Southern Vermont Art Center**—The center is open from June through mid-October Tuesday through Sun-

day. (Also on July 4 and Columbus Day.) After viewing the
changing exhibits by local artists, take a walk in the sculpture garden or on the botany trail, or have lunch in the
attractive garden café where the menu changes daily.
Lunch entrées are in the $8 range. Admission to the cen-
ter is $3 for adults, $.50 for students, children under 13
free. To get to the center, follow signs from Route 7A just
south of Manchester Center.

▲▲**Hildene**—This stucco Georgian revival mansion just
south of Manchester Village on Route 7A was built and
owned by Robert Todd Lincoln, son of Abraham Lincoln.
Hildene remained in the Lincoln family until 1975 and is
now open to the public. The furnishings, including a
1,000-pipe player organ complete with over 240 rolls of
music and a stove-pipe hat worn by the president, belonged to the Lincolns. Beautifully set in the Manchester
valley, Hildene's expansive front lawn was used as a driving range by avid golfer Robert Todd Lincoln. The estate's
formal English-style gardens were designed by his daughter Jesse, after she returned from England. Many special
events such as polo, symphony concerts, sleigh rides, and
cross-country skiing take place on the estate's "meadowlands." Even though the home is only open for tours from
mid-May through October, you may want to call (802)
362-1788 to see if there are any special goings-on should
your visit happen to fall in the off-season. Christmas
candlelight tours are especially popular. Admission to the
house is $5 for adults, $2 for children 6 to 15, children
under 6 are free. The last tour of the day leaves at 4:00 p.m.

▲**Norman Rockwell Exhibition and Gift Shop**—
More a gift shop than a museum, this place on 7A in
Arlington has hundreds of Rockwell magazine covers on
display but no original work. There is a film presentation
on the artist. Admission is $1 and the shop is open daily
from 9:00 a.m. to 7:00 p.m. I prefer the Rockwell
Museum in Stockbridge, Massachusetts, which you can
visit two days hence.

▲**Sky Line Drive**—For better views of the Green Mountains, take the 5.2-mile-long Sky Line Drive (toll road) to

the top of Mt. Equinox, the highest peak in the Taconic range. The drive is well worth taking on a clear day and is particularly dramatic at the height of fall foliage. There are a number of picnic areas and hiking trails on the way up and an inn at the 3,835-foot summit, but despite the view, you're better off opting for accommodations down in the village. The toll is $6 per car, and the drive is open from 8:00 a.m. to 10:00 p.m. daily, May 1 to November 1. Entrance to the auto road is on Route 7A south of Manchester Village.

Lodging and Dining

Reservations for the Manchester area are strongly advised, especially on weekends and during leaf-peeping season. At the Equinox, for example, rooms are often completely booked as much as six months in advance for peak foliage weekends. Some lodging establishments do have minimum stay requirements of two nights or more during high season, so be sure to check ahead of time.

The majestic **Equinox Hotel Resort and Spa** reigns supreme over historic Manchester Village. The historic hotel has recently been renovated and now serves as a 175-room resort. The grand exterior appears to stretch endlessly, as do the marble sidewalks that surround the building. Carriage rides are available from the hotel's doorstep. Rooms in season will run over $120 per night for two. For extra pampering, you may want to make use of the resort's spa facilities. Call (802) 362-4700 for reservations. Dinner entrées in the hotel's main dining room range from $16 to $24, with "lighter entrées" (really expanded portions of appetizers) ranging from $8.25 to $12.75. **Marsh Tavern** at the hotel has a buffet luncheon, dinner entrées from hamburgers to basil linguini ($8.95-$15), and evening entertainment.

The Reluctant Panther on West Road right in Manchester Village (802-362-2568 or 1-800-822-2331) has pleasing lodging and dining facilities. Rooms range from $95 to $150, and suites from $145 to $195 with continental breakfast included. The inn's restaurant features hearty soups, stews, and pies in the winter and lighter fare such as seafood and grilled dishes during the summer.

The 1811 House (802-362-1811), also in the village center, became an inn in 1811 but was it built in the 1770s. Authentically furnished with fine antiques, the house is on the National Register of Historic Places and once belonged to Mary Lincoln Isham, President Lincoln's granddaughter. Doubles run from $100 to $170 including a full breakfast (a two-night minimum stay is required on weekends, during fall foliage, and on holidays). There is a pub on the premises (open from 5:00 p.m. to 7:30 p.m.). **The Inn at Manchester,** just down the street on Route 7A toward Manchester Center, is open all year and serves a complete breakfast. Rates range from $65 to $165. Call (802) 362-1793 for reservations. The **Seth Warner Inn** (802-362-3830), also on 7A, has sunny rooms with country furnishings ($80 for two including breakfast).

For more of a retreat, try the **Birch Hill Inn** exquisitely set in the Vermont countryside several miles from town on West Road. The inn has a private trout pond and outdoor swimming pool. Dinner is $17 per person. Accommodations start at $49 per person including breakfast. Call (802) 362-2761 for reservations. The hosts and guests dine together on Monday, Tuesday, Friday, and Saturday evenings. Main courses such as veal marsala, pork tenderloin, chicken parmesan, cornish game hens, and beefalo specialties (made with beefalo from the farm next door) are always accompanied by soup, two vegetables, a potato or rice dish, wine, and dessert.

There are many motels in the vicinity of Manchester. Most of them are located on the outskirts of town on Routes 30, 7, and 7A. One of the nicest is the **North Shire** on 7A on the south side of the village. Rooms are spacious and attractively furnished and have lovely mountain views. The outdoor pool is pleasant, as are the helpful hosts who are more than willing to provide you with sightseeing and dining suggestions. Doubles are $58 to $75 per day including continental breakfast (802-362-2336).

If your lodging establishment doesn't serve food, the Manchester area has plenty of restaurants to satisfy just about any food craving. For breakfast, try **Up For Breakfast** on Main Street in Manchester Center, where breakfast dishes are far from ordinary ($4.25-$7.25). Or indulge in pancakes at **The Pancake House** just south of the Route 7/Route 30 junction. **The Park Bench**, also on Route 7, is nearby and is popular for lunch. **Christo's** next to Up For Breakfast features pizza and pasta at moderate prices ($5-$7.95). For dessert, the aroma from the **Cookie House** is hard to resist, while Vermont's own **Ben & Jerry's** ice cream shop just a couple of doors away will not do much to thin one's waistline either. **The Black Swan** (802-362-3807) on Route 7 between Manchester Center and the historic Village is renowned for fine dining, as is the **Arlington Inn** (802-375-6532) on Route 7A in nearby Arlington.

If you want to ship home some of Vermont's celebrated cheddar cheese, the Grand Union supermarket in Manchester Center is one of the best places in the area to purchase it. They have the cheese already packed for shipping, and their prices tend to be lower than elsewhere. The supermarket is also a good place to purchase Vermont maple syrup and prepared salads for picnicking.

Camping
Emerald Lake State Park, in East Dorset about 8 miles north of Manchester Center on US 7, has camping, swimming, a nature trail, and boating on a beautiful green lake that lives up to its name. The camping area has 105 sites, no hookups, 35 lean-tos, bathrooms, and pay showers. Canoes and rowboats can be rented for an outing on the lake. Call (802) 362-1655 for reservations.

Camping on the Battenkill is a private campground with both tent and RV sites, plus swimming and fishing on the Battenkill River. The campground, located on Route 7A in Arlington, is open from mid-April through October. Rates are $12.50 to $15.50 per campsite. Call (802) 375-6663 for reservations.

Nightlife

During June, July, and August, one can enjoy summer stock productions at the **Dorset Playhouse** on Route 30 5 miles north of Manchester Center. Call (802) 867-2223 for ticket information.

Itinerary Options

The Battenkill River, running from Manchester southwest through Arlington, is frequented by canoeists. **Battenkill Canoe Ltd.** at 1 River Road in Arlington can outfit you with the canoe trip of your choice. Contact them at (802) 375-9559 for additional information.

Battenkill Sports Bicycle Shop at the junction of Routes 7 and 30 in Manchester Center can fix you up with a mountain or touring bike for exploring the beautiful surrounding countryside. Call (802) 362-2734 for rental information.

Lake George, New York, a very popular lake resort, is only 43 miles from Rutland. To get there, continue on US 4 west from Rutland to Fort Ann. Then take Route 149 west to US 9 and follow it north to the town of Lake George.

Fort Ticonderoga, about 50 miles northwest of Rutland at Ticonderoga, New York, is also a popular tourist destination. To get to the fort, continue on US 4 west at Rutland to Whitehall, then take Route 22 north to Ticonderoga. The fort is open daily from mid-May through mid-October from 9:00 a.m. to 5:00 p.m., and until 6:00 p.m. during July and August. Admission is $6 for adults, $4 for children 10 to 13, children under 10 free.

BENNINGTON AND THE BERKSHIRES

Bennington, Vermont, was the site of a major Revolutionary War victory for the colonists in 1777. Today, looking at Old Bennington's graceful homes it is hard to believe that a war ever took place there.

Suggested Schedule

8:00 a.m.	Breakfast.
9:00 a.m.	Travel to Bennington and visit the Bennington Monument and Museum.
12:00 noon	Leave for Williamstown, Massachusetts.
12:30 p.m.	Lunch in Williamstown.
1:30 p.m.	Spend the afternoon exploring the Clark Institute and the Williams College art museum.
6:00 p.m.	Check into your Berkshire accommodation, your home base for the next two nights.

Travel Route: Manchester to Stockbridge/Lenox (75 miles)

From the Manchester area, continue on Route 7A south to Bennington. Covered bridge enthusiasts should make a short detour at Arlington to Route 313 where there are covered bridges on both sides of 7A. Farther along Route 7A, take Route 67 west at South Shaftsbury to Route 67A in North Bennington. There are two more covered bridges in quick succession along Route 67A as you approach Old Bennington.

Within Bennington itself, driving is confusing because roads are not well marked and route signs seem to contradict one another. The easiest way to get your bearings is to look for the Bennington Monument, which stands high on the hill above the town, and drive toward it. At the monument ask directions to the museum.

Leaving Bennington, take US 7 south, stopping in

The Berkshires

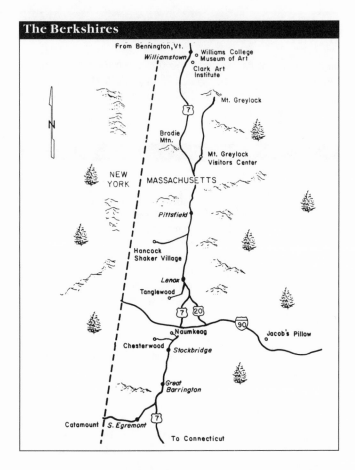

Williamstown for the afternoon, then continue on US 7 to Lenox and Stockbridge in the heart of the Berkshire region.

Bennington Sightseeing Highlights

▲▲**The Bennington Museum**—The primary reason for visiting this museum, approximately one-half mile from the Bennington Monument on Route 9, is its collection of works by famed American folk artist Grandma Moses, who continued to be productive well into her nineties. The museum's collection also includes early American furniture, glassware, pottery, military artifacts, and household items such as pedal-operated sewing machines. The museum is open daily from 9:00 a.m. to 5:00 p.m. March 1 through December 23 except for Thanksgiving Day. January 2 through February 28 it is open on weekends and holidays only. Admission is $4.50 for adults, $3.50 for students and senior citizens, children under 12 are free. Family admission for two adults and two children under 18 is $10.

▲**The Bennington Monument**—Completed in 1891, the monument commemorates the Battle of Bennington and is the centerpiece of lovely Old Bennington. It warrants a visit on any clear day for the view, and it is a must at the height of fall foliage season. You can see three states—Massachusetts, New York, and Vermont—from the observation deck. An elevator takes you to the top of the 306-foot structure, so there is no stair-climbing involved. A small admission fee is charged. The well-groomed houses that line the road leading to and from the monument are worth a look as well.

The Old First Church—Adjacent to the Town Green in Old Bennington, this is a lovely example of early nineteenth-century church architecture in New England. Perhaps more interesting, though, is its graveyard with headstones dating back to the Revolutionary War. Poet Robert Frost is buried here.

▲**Park-McCullough House**—If you have time, you may want to visit this lovely 35-room Victorian mansion in North Bennington. Once home to two Vermont governors, the house is filled with family antiques and beautiful details such as a stained-glass skylight and intricately patterned frosted-glass light fixtures. The house is open for tours from early May through October 10:00 a.m. to 4:00 p.m., with the last tour leaving at 3:00 p.m. Admission is $3 for adults, $2.50 for seniors, $1.50 for youths 12 to 17. Special "Victorian Christmas" tours are run during the holidays. Call (802) 442-5441 for a schedule.

Williamstown Sightseeing Highlights

In this quintessential college town, Williams College dominates just about every aspect of town life, providing the residents of this sleepy Berkshire community with a wealth of cultural activities that many rural communities lack, including two outstanding art museums.

▲▲▲**Sterling & Francine Clark Art Institute**—The museum has room after room of stunning French impressionist paintings, Renoir and Monet among others, and works by noted American painters such as Homer, Cassatt, and Sargent. The fine collection also includes English silver and works dating back to the fifteenth century. Admission is free. Open 10.00 a.m. to 5:00 p.m. Tuesday through Sunday. Closed on Thanksgiving, Christmas, and New Year's Day. The museum is open Memorial, Labor, and Columbus days.

▲▲**Williams College Art Museum**—The museum's collection ranges from ancient Greek vases to Andy Warhol pop art. There is also a gallery devoted to the artist brothers, Maurice and Charles Prendergast. Admission is free. Open 10:00 a.m. to 5:00 p.m. Monday through Saturday, and Sunday from 1:00 to 5:00 p.m. The museum is closed for Thanksgiving, Christmas, and New Year's Day.

▲**The Williamstown Theatre Festival**—The festival is widely known for its high-quality summer productions. Many popular actors got their start here, and some return on occasion to hone their stage skills. Call (413) 597-3400 for performance and ticket information.

Lodging and Dining

You can find comfortable lodging at the **Williams Inn** (413-458-9371) on the Green in Williamstown if you plan to stay for a performance at the playhouse. If you're not attending the theater, I suggest putting up for the next two nights in Stockbridge or Lenox, both better jumping-off points for Berkshire activities.

The Red Lion Inn in Stockbridge is one of the best-known inns in the area and deservedly so. The Red Lion, the focal point of the town, has been treating its guests regally for over 200 years. Double rooms at the inn start around $90 in peak season (May through October). Singles and two-room suites are also available. Call (413) 298-5545 for reservations. If you are unable to book a room here, at least partake of a traditional New England meal such as prime rib, stuffed lobster, or scrod in the main dining room; or people-watch while sipping cocktails on the inn's front porch. **The Lion's Den** downstairs has pub fare and entertainment in the evenings.

There are two pleasant inns in the quiet town of South Lee, once a mill town, about a mile and a half from Stockbridge. **The Merrell Tavern Inn**, built in 1794, has the only remaining colonial circular bar in America. Rooms are furnished with antiques, and the property borders on the Housatonic River. Double rooms including an ample breakfast range from $55 to $130 per night (413-243-1794). Just across the street, the **Federal House**, known locally for its fine European cuisine, also rents rooms to overnight guests. Call (413) 243-1824 for dining or lodging reservations.

Lovely Lenox has its share of attractive inns right in the center of town on Walker Street. Each guest room in the **Walker House** is named after a famous composer and is furnished accordingly. Guests are welcome to use the inn's delightful porches or watch movies in the library. The hosts are warm and friendly, and breakfast and afternoon tea are included in the room rates of $50 to $130 (413-637-1271). **The Gables Inn** just down the street was once the home of Edith Wharton. Rooms here are also thematic—the Shakespeare room, the Show Business room, and the Presidential room with pictures and memorabilia of past presidents. Rates, including continental breakfast at an elegantly set table, are $60 to $175 per night depending on the season and type of room. There's also a pool on the premises. Call (413) 637-3416.

Two other inns on Walker Street have restaurants and overnight accommodations. **Gateways Inn and Restaurant** has four large suites with private baths, fireplaces, and curly maple furniture for $90 to $295 (413-637-2532). Prix fixe dinners at $27.50 per person feature dishes such as breast of chicken topped with crawfish, truffle and cèpes served in a honey liqueur sauce, and medallions of monkfish stuffed with Norwegian salmon and topped with a fresh basil sauce. The menu at the **Candlelight**

Inn changes seasonally but is primarily continental and
American in focus. Dinner entrées range from $17.95 to
$24.95, and lunch generally runs $4.95 to $14.95. Try the
Chocolate Chippie for dessert. Upstairs rooms range from
$60 to $155 per night (413-637-1555).

Outside Lenox, a turreted estate has been turned into
one of the most elegant lodging establishments around.
Set on 85 acres, and restored by the owners of the Red
Lion Inn, **Blantyre** is truly a feast for the eyes. You'll
have to have a deep pocketbook to stay there, however, as
rooms average about $250 per night—tennis and con-
tinental breakfast included.

Somewhat more affordable are the strip of motels on
US 7 between Pittsfield and Lenox, including the **Suisse
Chalet** where a double room goes for about $45 a night
(413-637-3560 or 1-800-258-1980). More motels can also
be found on US 7 between Stockbridge and Great Barrington. The area abounds with country inns, but accommodations do fill up quickly on weekends so you may
want to call the Berkshire Visitor's Bureau at (413)
443-9186 for a complete lodging list.

For less formal dining options than listed above,
Michael's on Elm Street in Stockbridge serves a variety
of American dishes, with dinner prices ranging from $7
to $16. For gourmet takeout or eat-in pasta salads, try **La
Fete Chez Vous** down an alley off Main Street between
the Red Lion and Elm Street. **The Cafe** in the mews
behind the Red Lion also serves salads and sandwiches
for about $5.

Camping
The **Pittsfield State Forest** (413-442-8992) has 31 campsites, and **October Mountain State Forest** (413-243-1778)
in Lee has 50. The campground at October Mountain is
more convenient for sightseeing, so reservations are
strongly recommended. Sites are about $12 per night.
Both campgrounds have bathrooms with wheelchair
access and are open seasonally. **Bonnie Brae Cabins
and Campsites** at Pontoosuc Lake just off US 7 several

miles north of downtown Pittsfield might also be an economical alternative to staying in a country inn. Open May
through October, Bonnie Brae has cabins that rent for
$30 to $52 per night, and campsites go for about $19 per
night. Call (413) 442-3754 for information.

Itinerary Options
If you would prefer to spend your day outdoors, take the
scenic drive over Mt. Greylock. On fair days the view
of the Berkshires is extraordinary. The entrance to the
visitors center is off US 7 just south of New Ashford.

Horse-racing fans traveling this route in August may
want to take a 35-mile detour from Arlington, Vermont,
to Saratoga Springs, New York. In addition to being recognized for thoroughbred horse-racing and natural springs,
Saratoga also has fine homes in its favor. **The National
Museum of Racing and Thoroughbred Hall of Fame**
is in Saratoga, as well as the unusual **Petrified Sea
Gardens**.

Historic Deerfield
Deerfield, about 35 miles southeast of Williamstown,
Massachusetts, is one of the most perfectly preserved
historic towns in New England. While many of the buildings are privately owned by either individuals or Deerfield Academy, twelve of them are open to the public and
can be toured with one admission ticket. Guided tours of
the houses last thirty minutes each, so you'll need a full
day if you want to visit them all. Tickets are $7.50 for
adults, $4 for children 6 to 17, and can be purchased at
the information center on the village's main street (called
The Street). The buildings are open daily from 9:30 a.m.
to 4:30 p.m. except Thanksgiving, Christmas Eve, and
Christmas.

In addition to the historic houses, **The Memorial Hall
Museum** on Memorial Street in the center of Deerfield
has period rooms including a Victorian bedroom and a
colonial kitchen. Indian artifacts and pottery, handmade
quilts, and nineteenth-century clothing are also on dis-

play. The museum is open weekdays from 10:00 a.m. to 4:30 p.m., Saturday and Sunday from 12:30 p.m. to 4:30 p.m. May 1 through October 31. Admission is $2.50 for adults, $1.50 for students, $.75 for children 6 to 12. The grounds of lovely Deerfield Academy are also worth strolling through.

If you do plan to stay at Deerfield for the day, there are picnic tables behind the information center. **The Deerfield Inn** right across the street from the information center is a fine lodging and dining establishment. Lunch entrées such as shrimp scampi, oriental chicken, and seafood casserole range from $8.75 to $10.25. Pheasant, veal with wild mushrooms, and venison dishes are just a sampling of the varied dinner menu, priced from $17 to $23. Overnight accommodations including breakfast start at $60 per person. Call (413) 774-5587 for reservations.

To get to Deerfield, take Route 2 east from Williamstown to Greenfield. From Greenfield, follow US 5 south to Deerfield.

THE BERKSHIRES

Because the Berkshires offer the visitor so much in the way of outdoor recreation, such as golf, skiing, and hiking, cultural events such as the Boston Symphony Orchestra at Tanglewood, picturesque villages such as Stockbridge, and of course the beauty of the Berkshire hills themselves, the area has been a popular resort for over a hundred years. Couple the attractions with the fact that the Berkshires are only three hours from both New York City and Boston, and it is amazing that the area is not overrun with souvenir shop malls, factory outlets, and T-shirt shops designed to take advantage of the tourist dollar. Fortunately, due to careful planning, most towns remain much as they were when Norman Rockwell painted here in the 1950s, and many have changed little in the last century.

Suggested Schedule

9:00 a.m.	Breakfast.
10:00 a.m.	Visit Hancock Shaker Village.
12:30 p.m.	Lunch.
1:30 p.m.	Tour Chesterwood.
3:30 p.m.	Visit the Norman Rockwell Museum.
4:30 p.m.	Stroll down Main Street in Stockbridge, perhaps stopping at the Red Lion for tea or a cocktail and people-watching.
6:00 p.m.	Dinner.
8:00 p.m.	Take in an evening performance of the entertainment of your choice.

Travel Route

Travel to Hancock Shaker Village at the junction of US 20 and Route 41 about 12 miles northwest of Stockbridge. From the village you'll take Route 41 south to Route 102 east, following it until it intersects with Route 183 south. Take Route 183 south and follow signs to Chesterwood. After leaving Chesterwood, retrace your steps back to

Route 102, and continue on Route 102 east for two miles into Stockbridge Center. The tourist information booth on Main Street in Stockbridge can provide you with directions to other area points of interest, and in most cases, sights are well marked by directional signs.

Sightseeing Highlights

▲▲▲ **Hancock Shaker Village**—Allow at least two hours to explore this village, one of the best examples of the everyday life of an unusual religious sect called the Shakers. There are live demonstrations of Shaker crafts such as broom making and basket weaving. Two 60-minute tours daily at 10:30 a.m. and 2:00 p.m. take you through part of the village. If you are unable to time your visit for a guided tour, you are free to tour the complex on your own. The descriptive panels in each room describe different aspects of Shaker life. Don't miss the unique round barn. The village is open daily from April through November. The hours are 9:30 a.m. to 5:00 p.m. Memorial Day weekend through October, 10:00 a.m. to 3:00 p.m. during April, May, and November. The village is located at the junction of Routes 41 and 20 in Hancock. There are picnic tables outside the visitor center. Entrance fees are $8 for adults, $7.25 for students and seniors, $4 for children 6 to 12, and $22 for families.

▲▲**Chesterwood**—This was the summer home of sculptor Daniel Chester French, who is known for the Lincoln Memorial in Washington and the Minute Man statue in Concord, Massachusetts, as well as many other works that adorn governmental buildings. Plaster castings of his works are displayed in his barn, home, and studio. Many of his works were so large he had to transport them out of his studio on railroad tracks just to see how they'd look in the sunlight. Each summer, usually beginning July 4th weekend, contemporary sculpture from local artists is on exhibit throughout the grounds and along the nature trail. Chesterwood is operated by the National Trust and is open daily May through October from 10:00 a.m. to 5:00 p.m. There is a picnic area next to the parking lot. Admission is $5 for adults, $1 for children ages 6 to 18.

▲▲**The Norman Rockwell Museum**—This museum is housed in "The Old Corner House" on Main Street in Stockbridge. Rockwell fans will enjoy this small but choice collection. Those previously indifferent to Rockwell will become converts when they witness the clarity and vitality of his oils firsthand. Open daily from 10:00 a.m. to 5:00 p.m. May through October. November through April the museum is open Monday through Friday from 11:00 a.m. to 4:00 p.m., and on Saturday and Sunday from 10:00 a.m. to 5:00 p.m. It is closed on Christmas, Thanksgiving, and New Year's Day, and for ten days in January. Admission is $5 for adults, $1 for children 6 to 18.

▲**The Berkshire Garden Center**—This 15-acre botanic garden off Route 102, just before you come to the intersection of Route 183, is a nice spot for a picnic lunch between visits to Hancock Shaker Village and Chesterwood. The center is open daily from 10:00 a.m. to 5:00 p.m. The greenhouses are open year-round, while the gardens may be toured May through October, and admission is charged during those months (somewhat pricey for a botanic garden of this size, the garden is run by a nonprofit organization). Admission is $4 for adults, $3 for seniors, $1 for children 6 to 12, and family admission is $10.

▲**Naumkeag**—Designed by Stanford White, this stately brick and shingle home open to the public is about one-half mile from the Red Lion Inn on Prospect Hill Road. The formal gardens are open from 10:00 a.m. to 5:00 p.m. during the summer. The house may be toured Tuesday through Sunday beginning at 10:00 a.m. with the last tour leaving at 4:15 p.m. Admission to the house and gardens is $5, admission to the house alone is $4, and garden admission only is $3. Open daily Memorial Day through Labor Day, and on weekends and holidays from Labor Day through Columbus Day.

▲**The Mount**—Off US 7 between Lenox and Stockbridge, this was the summer estate of American novelist Edith Wharton. Perhaps her most famous novel, *Ethan Frome*, was set in Lenox. Visitors can tour the property during the summer months. Admission is charged. Plays

based on the author's works are presented here during
July and August. Tickets to the matinee performances
include afternoon tea. Call (413) 637-1899 for complete
details.

▲**Arrowhead**—Author Herman Melville made his home
here for thirteen years during the mid-1800s. See the
room where Melville penned *Moby Dick* and several
other novels. Located on Holmes Road in Pittsfield, Arrowhead is open for guided tours Memorial Day through
October. The hours are 10:00 a.m. to 4:30 a.m. Monday
through Saturday, and Sunday from 11:00 a.m. to 3:30 p.m.
After Labor Day the museum is closed on Tuesday and
Wednesday. Admission is $3.50 for adults, $3 for seniors,
and $2 for children 6 to 16.

▲**The Berkshire Museum**—The museum is a combination art and natural history museum. Its collections
include everything from gemstones to piranhas to boa
constrictors to a fine selection of landscapes by artists of
the Hudson River School. Located at 39 South Street on
US 7 in Pittsfield, the museum is open Tuesday through
Saturday from 10:00 a.m. to 5:00 p.m., and Sunday from
1:00 p.m. to 5:00 p.m. During July and August, it is also
open on Monday from 10:00 a.m. to 5:00 p.m. Admission
is free, but donations are greatly appreciated.

Other Sights—There are several historic homes in
Stockbridge that visitors can tour during the summer
months. **The Mission House Museum** on West Main
Street in Stockbridge was built in 1739 for the Reverend
John Sargeant, the first missionary to the Stockbridge
Indians. The house originally stood on the hill overlook-
ing town but was moved to its present location in 1926.
Tours of the house and garden run Tuesday through Sun-
day from 11:00 a.m. to 4:00 p.m. Memorial Day weekend
through Columbus Day. Admission is $3.50 for adults,
$1 for children 6 to 12. Diagonally across the street is the
Merwin House, which can be toured June 1 through
October 15 on Tuesday, Thursday, Saturday, and Sunday
from 1:00 to 5:00 p.m.

Train buffs may wish to visit the **Berkshire Scenic
Railway Museum** in Lenox. Call (413) 637-2210 for

ticket and schedule information if you're interested in taking the train ride along the Housatonic River. The museum is open weekends and holidays June through October. Admission is free.

In Great Barrington, south of Stockbridge, the **Albert Schweitzer Center** is a museum and library dedicated to Dr. Schweitzer. There is a wildlife sanctuary on the grounds. The center is open Tuesday through Saturday from 10:00 a.m. to 4:00 p.m., and Sunday from noon to 4:00 p.m. Donations are requested.

Performing Arts

A visit to **Tanglewood**, the Boston Symphony Orchestra's summer home in Lenox, is the favorite form of night-time entertainment in the Berkshires. The BSO performs in the "Shed" on lovely wooded grounds. Tickets are available for seating in the Shed, but on clear nights Beethoven is best heard with a champagne picnic on the lawn. Bring your own blanket and dress warmly. Early birds can catch afternoon rehearsal performances at bargain prices. Call the box office at (413) 637-1940 for information during the summer months. In the off-season, you'll need to contact the BSO's office in Boston, (617) 266-1492, for details. Tanglewood is located off Route 183 about two miles south of Lenox Center.

Jacob's Pillow is also a popular summer cultural event. The dance festival features various well-known and talented traveling dance troupes. The Pillow is located in Becket on US 20 about eight miles from Lee. Call (413) 243-0745 for schedule and tickets.

Other cultural events in the area include **The Berkshire Theatre Festival** in Stockbridge (413-298-5576), **The Berkshire Ballet** in Pittsfield (413-442-1307), **The Berkshire Opera Company** (413-243-1343), and **The Berkshire Public Theatre** in Pittsfield (413-445-4634).

The Berkshire Ticket Booth at the Chamber Office in the Lenox Academy building at 75 Main Street in Lenox sells tickets to area events. The booth is open Monday through Saturday from 1:00 to 5:00 p.m.; it sells same-day discounted tickets whenever they are available.

Itinerary Option

From the Berkshires, it is only a two-hour drive to the Catskill mountains in New York state. The Catskills are somewhat less traveled during fall foliage than most of New England, but the scenery is no less spectacular.

To get there, follow US 7 south to Great Barrington. From Great Barrington, follow Route 23 west to Hudson, New York. At Hudson, cross the Rip Van Winkle Bridge to Catskill, New York.

CONNECTICUT RIVER VALLEY

Leaving the Berkshires behind, you'll be exposed to a
castle, a capital, and culture as you travel along the Connecticut River today.

Suggested Schedule

8:00 a.m.	Have breakfast and leave the Berkshires.
10:30 a.m.	Tour Nook Farm.
12:30 p.m.	Lunch in Hartford or picnic along the Connecticut River.
2:30 p.m.	Visit Gillette's Castle.
4:00 p.m.	Amble along Essex's Main Street.
5:00 p.m.	Have an early dinner or late afternoon snack at the Griswold Inn.
6:00 p.m.	Head on up the coast to settle in for the night in Mystic.

Travel Route: Stockbridge to Mystic (110 miles)

From Stockbridge, head south on US 7 through the
antique-lovers' havens of South Egremont and Sheffield.
At Canaan, take US 44 east. After entering West Hartford,
turn right onto Prospect. Then after about five minutes,
turn left on Farmington Avenue. The parking lot for the
Stowe and Twain houses is on your right immediately
after the Woodland Street stoplight.

Alternative Route to Hartford: If you have extra
time, a more scenic route from the Berkshires to Hartford
is through the northwestern corner of Connecticut,
which many consider the prettiest part of the state.
Instead of turning east at Canaan, continue on US 7 south
to Kent, passing through West Cornwall where there is a
covered bridge. From Kent, take Route 341 east through
Warren to Woodville. At Woodville, go east on US 202 to
Litchfield, a showplace for exquisite eighteenth-century
estates. The Congregational church on Litchfield's village
green is widely noted for its classic New England
architecture. Leaving Litchfield, take Route 118 east to

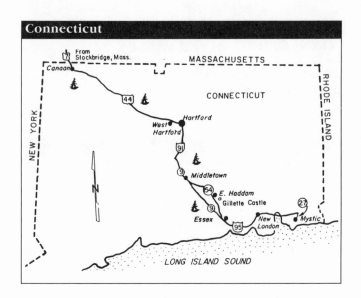

Route 4, then follow 4 east to West Hartford. Art lovers
following this alternate route should visit the **Hill-Stead
Museum** in Farmington, originally designed as a private
home by architect Stanford White. The house is now
filled with choice furnishings and impressionist paintings. Call (203) 677-4787 for hours of operation and
admission charges. The museum is closed from mid-
January to mid-February.

From Hartford, take Interstate 84 east to Interstate 91
south. Exit I-91 south at Route 9 south and pass by Middletown, home of Wesleyan University. At Exit 10 take
Route 154 south. A good place to picnic is Haddam
Meadows State Park right along the river just off this highway. To visit the Goodspeed Opera House and Gillette's
Castle, take Route 82 east and follow signs to both.

After conquering the castle, retrace your steps to Route
154 south to get to Essex, an attractive town whose past
and present have been shaped by nautical endeavors. In
1814, during the War of 1812, the British raided Essex and
burned many of the town's ships, causing great hardship
to the townspeople. Today, well-kept houses are dis-
creetly tucked away on the waterfront, while the marina
is filled with pleasure craft. From Essex, take Route 154

south to the intersection with Route 9, then take Route 9
south to Interstate 95 north, getting off at the Mystic Exit,
#90 (Route 27).

Sightseeing Highlights
▲▲▲**Nook Farm**—Only a handful of houses remain
from this nineteenth-century community for the literary
elite of Hartford. Two are open to the public and worth
seeing: the homes of Harriet Beecher Stowe and Samuel
Clemens (Mark Twain). The Beecher Stowe house exemplifies a conventional upper-middle-class Victorian
home, whereas the more pretentious Twain house is a
monument to his eccentricities. In both cases, many of
the writers' personal effects have been preserved. Among
them, Stowe's original paintings and Twain's bed and the
dining room chair from which he told fantastic tales to
his guests and family. Tour guides recount humorous
details from the authors' everyday lives. The guided tour
of both homes takes approximately an hour and fifteen
minutes. Admission is charged. Nook Farm is open June 1
through Columbus Day, and the month of December,
Monday through Saturday from 9:30 a.m. to 4:00 p.m.,
Sunday from noon to 4:00 p.m. Hours the rest of the year
are 9:30 a.m. to 4:00 p.m. Tuesday through Saturday, and
12:00 p.m. to 4:00 p.m. on Sunday. If you're ready for
lunch after Nook Farm, drive one mile into Hartford's
center. The best selection of restaurants is found along
Main Street.
Goodspeed's Opera House—Somewhat of an area
landmark, this attractive building on the banks of the
Connecticut River in East Haddam will catch your eye on
the way to Gillette's Castle. Tours are available, and,
should you decide to stay in the area a while, the opera
house hosts evening performances of popular musicals
April through December. You can picnic on the river's
edge prior to a show. Call (203) 873-8668 for schedule
and ticket information.
▲▲**Gillette's Castle**—They say a man's home is his castle, and in actor William Gillette's case, that statement can

be taken literally. Best known for his portrayal of Sher-
lock Holmes, Gillette built his castle overlooking the
Connecticut River in Hadlyme. The jagged stone exterior
is striking, but except for several intricately carved
wooden doors, the interior is fairly modest. Children will
no doubt enjoy exploring the castle, and theater buffs
will appreciate the Broadway memorabilia on display.
Admission, $1 for adults and $.50 for children 6 to 11, is
reasonable and won't break the family pocketbook. The
castle grounds are a Connecticut state park, so there are
picnic tables available as well as a souvenir shop and
refreshment stand. Skip the wooded trail unless you are
in the mood to stretch your legs. The castle is open daily
from Memorial Day through Columbus Day 11:00 a.m. to
5:00 p.m., and on weekends only Columbus Day through
mid-December from 10:00 a.m. to 4:00 p.m.

▲**Connecticut River Museum**—On the waterfront at
the end of Main Street in Essex, the museum's exhibits
pertain to river history. The museum is open April through
December, Tuesday through Sunday from 10:00 a.m. to
5:00 p.m. Admission is $2.50 for adults, and children
under 12 free.

▲▲**Steam Train and Riverboat Ride**—On Railroad
Avenue in Essex, this excursion offers a good alternative
way to see the Connecticut River and sights such as
Gillette's Castle and Goodspeed's Opera House if you're
tired of driving or if you fancy steam-powered locomo-
tives. All trains connect with a riverboat cruise, except
the last one of the day. Tickets cost $12.95 for adults,
$5.95 for children 2 and older, children under 2 free, for
the combined train and riverboat trip, less for the train
ride only. The combined trip takes over two hours; separate tickets are not sold for the riverboat cruise. The service
operates May through October. Call ahead for departure
times as they vary from day to day and from season to
season, (203) 767-0103.

Lodging
The Tourist Information Center at the Mystic exit will
help you find lodging. There is a board listing nearby

accommodations, their rates, and driving distances. The center's helpful personnel will even call ahead to secure your room. While there, be sure to peruse the menus from area restaurants and pick out the ones that best suit your tastes and budget. The tourist center is also a great source of area sightseeing information.

The Inn at Mystic, at the junction of Routes 27 and US 1, has accommodations ranging from motor court rooms to comfortable rooms in a traditional country inn. There are gardens, a tennis court, a restaurant, a pool, and a hot tub on the premises. Rooms in the motor court are $85 to $135 during the summer, and $65 to $85 off-season. Rooms at the inn go for $155 to $185 per night. Call (1-800) 237-2415 or (203) 536-9604 for reservations.

If you wish to stay within walking distance of Mystic's downtown shops and restaurants, **The Whaler's Inn,** offering simple, motellike accommodations and senior citizen discounts, is your only lodging choice in Mystic center. Doubles range from $55 to $110 per night. Call (203) 536-1506 or (1-800) 243-2588.

Camping
Seaport Campground, 3 miles from Mystic Seaport Museum, is the closest campground to Mystic's attractions. From Exit 90 on Interstate 95, take Route 27 north for one and a quarter miles to Route 184. Follow that east for about one-half mile and watch for the campground on your left. RV hookups and tent sites are available, as well as complete recreational facilities, including swimming, on the premises. Open seasonally, mid-April through late October. Call (203) 536-4044 for reservations.

Dining
The Griswold Inn, Essex, serves sandwiches and burgers for lunch and traditional New England fare for dinner in a lively atmosphere. A fine collection of firearms and maritime prints grace the walls of the Griswold's several dining rooms. Lunch is about $8 per person and dinner entrées run from $15 to $20. Servings are hearty. The inn also has 23 guest rooms. Reservations are recommended for overnight lodging or weekend dinners. Call (203) 767-0991.

In the Mystic area, you'll find a number of reasonably priced restaurants and fast-food establishments in and around Olde Mystick Village, just off I-95. In downtown Mystic, **Mulligan's**, on the west side of the drawbridge, has moderately priced meals ranging from sandwiches to lobster (203-536-2674). Locals recommend **The Draw Bridge Inne**, a half block from the drawbridge on Main Street, offering specialties for seafarers and landlubbers alike. Dinner entrées are $13 and up (401-536-9653).

For a simple but filling meal, try an overstuffed sandwich at **2 Sisters Deli** on Pearl Street just off Main. For breakfast, try **Bee Bee Dairy**, a family-style restaurant on Main Street, or **The Binnacle**, which has a very casual atmosphere and filling breakfasts.

Itinerary Option

Those who wish to extend their New England vacation southward to explore the exclusive Hamptons or sand dunes at Montauk can take the ferry from New London, Connecticut (several miles south of Mystic), to Orient Point on Long Island, New York. The ferry costs over $20 one-way for most automobiles including the driver, and you really do need to bring your car across to do any sightseeing. The ferry operates year-round except for Christmas Day. Sailing time is approximately one and a half hours. Call (203) 443-5281 for schedule and reservation information. From Orient Point, take Route 25 west to Riverhead where you pick up Route 24. Follow Route 24 until it intersects with Route 27. Drive east on Route 27 to the Hamptons, then continue all the way out to the lighthouse at Montauk Point.

MYSTIC

Early New Englanders were dependent on the ocean for food, fuel (in the form of whale oil for lanterns), and goods brought from abroad. The importance of the sea comes to life in Mystic Seaport's re-creation of a nineteenth-century maritime village.

Suggested Schedule

8:30 a.m.	Breakfast.
9:30 a.m.	Mystic Seaport Museum.
4:00 p.m.	Leave For Newport, Rhode Island.

Travel Route: Mystic to Newport (45 miles)

From Mystic center, travel along coastal US 1 to Route 138 east. Cross over to Jamestown, then take the Jamestown toll bridge to Newport. Several miles north of Mystic you may want to take a short detour on Route 1A to see the handsome village of Stonington.

Sightseeing Highlights

▲▲▲ **Mystic Seaport Museum**—The entrance to the village is on Route 27 east less than one mile from I-95. You'll need the better part of a day to explore the museum grounds fully. Climb aboard a whaling vessel to see the cramped quarters of deckhands and where whale blubber was processed; visit seaport shops typical of those that would have served a fishing community 100 years ago; watch boat builders at work; learn how fishermen navigated by the stars, in the planetarium; and see how sailing, once a necessary skill, has become a modern sport, in a special tribute to the America's Cup. General admission to the village, at $12.50 for adults, $6.25 for children 5 to 18, is rather expensive, but due to the vast number of exhibits the Seaport has to offer, the money is well spent. Separate tickets must be purchased if you wish to take one of the steamboat cruises that leave from the village or to visit the museum's planetarium. For a fast-food lunch of clam cakes, burgers, or hot dogs, there is a snack bar in the village; for more refined dining, try the **Seaman's Inne** next to the complex. The museum is open daily in the spring and summer from 9:00 a.m. to 5:00 p.m., in the fall and winter from 9:00 a.m. to 4:00 p.m., closed Christmas.

▲**Mystic Marinelife Aquarium**—Just off I-95 at the Mystic Exit, this is a worthwhile stop if you didn't make it to the New England Aquarium in Boston and have extra time after visiting the Seaport. Entrance fees are $7.25 for adults, $6.25 for seniors, $4.25 for children 5 to 17. The aquarium is open daily from 9:00 a.m. to 5:30 p.m. June 29 through Labor Day, and 9:00 a.m. to 4:40 p.m. during the rest of the year. It is closed Thanksgiving, Christmas, and New Year's Day.

▲**Denison Pequotsepos Nature Center**—The 125-acre center, on Pequotsepos Road in Mystic, is comprised of self-guided nature trails and a small natural history museum. One trail is designed especially for blind visitors. The center is open April through October, Monday through Saturday 8:00 a.m. to 4:00 p.m., Sunday 1:00 to 5:00 p.m. During the winter months it is open Tuesday through Saturday from 10:00 a.m. to 4:00 p.m., and Sunday 1:00 to 4:00 p.m. Admission is $1 for adults, $.50 for children over 6.

Olde Mystic Village—It is probably best to pass on this group of souvenir shops and informal eating establishments adjacent to the aquarium unless you have plenty of time to kill.

Newport Lodging
Stay in the heart of things at the **Inntowne** on the corner of Thames and Mary streets where many of the shops and restaurants of Newport are at your doorstep. Rates range from $55 to $160 depending on the season and type of accommodation. Call (401) 846-9200 for reservations.

The newly built **Marriott** on the waterfront is also convenient to Newport center. Nine of the Marriott's rooms

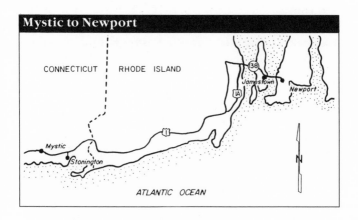

Mystic to Newport

CONNECTICUT | RHODE ISLAND

Jamestown   Newport

Mystic

Stonington

ATLANTIC OCEAN

N

are specially equipped for handicapped guests. Doubles run from about $145 to $220. Call Marriott's toll-free number, (1-800) 458-3066, or the hotel directly at (401) 849-1000.

Nearby, on quiet Clarke Street but still in the center of Newport, is a row of three bed and breakfast establishments. **The Queen Anne** at #16 was built in the Victorian era and offers reasonable accommodations with shared bath starting at $50 per night (401-846-5676). **The Admiral Farragut** (401-849-0640) at 31 Clarke was built in 1650. Their doubles range from $75 to $98 during the summer and start at $45 during the winter. Two of the nicest hosts in Newport, Sam and Rita Rogers, run **The Melville House** (401-847-0640) at 39 Clarke Street. The inn, built in 1750, is listed on the National Register of Historic Places. Doubles start at $40 in the winter and $70 in the summer, and breakfast is included.

For a splurge you won't soon forget, stay at the **Inn at Castle Hill** off Ocean Drive. With a room overlooking the ocean, you'll almost feel like a Vanderbilt. Doubles with a private bath and water view are $180 during the summer, significantly less during the winter months. The inn's restaurant is also well worth a try (401-849-3800).

Bed & Breakfast of Rhode Island (401-849-1298) can also help you locate accommodations. Their service is free of charge.

Camping

There are several municipal campgrounds near Newport, the closest being **Middletown Campground** on Second Beach in neighboring Middletown. Since there are only 44 campsites, reservations are strongly recommended. Call (401) 846-5781. Open May through early October. Facilities include toilets, showers, and sewer hookups.

On the far side of the island, **Melville Ponds Campground** off Route 114 in Portsmouth has tent sites, RV sites with hookups, and recreational facilities. Open April 1 through October 31. Call (401) 849-8212.

If all campgrounds on the island are filled, try the campground in Jamestown at **Fort Getty Recreation Area.** You can fish at the campground, but you will have to cross the toll bridge to sightsee in Newport. Open during the summer months; call (401) 423-1363 for reservation information.

Newport Dining

The Black Pearl (401-846-5264) on Bannister's Wharf is a very popular Newport restaurant, as evidenced by the throngs of hungry diners in line to be seated. Because of its reputation, the restaurant can be crowded and the service slow. Next door at the **Clarke Cooke House** (401-849-2900), you'll find truly elegant dining upstairs for dinner and a more casual atmosphere downstairs at **The Candy Store**. For dining in unique settings, try the **La Forge Restaurant** overlooking the grass courts at the Newport Casino, serving veal and chicken dinner entrées that run about $10; **The Moorings** situated in the famous New York Yacht Club on Sayer's Wharf (401-846-2260); or the **White Horse Tavern**, the oldest operating tavern in the United States (401-849-3600). Numerous restaurants along Thames Street offer cheaper alternatives for eating out.

For dessert, visit any one of **The Newport Creamery**'s several locations for a traditional ice cream cone. **Poor Richard's** at 254 Thames Street is the place to get breakfast, from pancakes to omelets.

Itinerary Option

Need a break from vigorous sightseeing? Need a break from the world in general? Then a trip to Block Island may just be the antidote. Only 12 miles off the coast of Rhode Island, Block Island was originally settled in 1661. The island offers visitors all of the quiet beauty, miles of beach, and dramatic cliffs of Martha's Vineyard, without the commercialism.

If you enjoy cycling past sand dunes, beach roses, lily ponds, and old stone walls, exploring wildlife refuges and lighthouses, or just lounging on the beach, Block Island will be a welcome retreat. But if you're looking for art museums, chic shops, and active nightlife, then this is not the place for you. There is only one town on the island, consisting primarily of one main street lined with Victorian era hotels and a handful of restaurants and souvenir shops.

Ferries to the island operate from Point Judith, Rhode Island, year-round, though a winter visit is not recommended. (To get to the ferry, travel north on US 1 from Mystic, and follow signs to Point Judith and the ferry.) Service is more frequent during the summer, and ferries even run from Newport during the summer months. The trip from Point Judith takes a little over an hour. One-way fares are $6.10 for adults, $3.15 for children, and $10 and $5, respectively, for a same-day round-trip. Passenger cars cost $20.25 one way, motorcycles are $11.85, and bicycles are $1.75. Call (401) 783-7328 or (401) 783-4613 for reservations and a current ferry schedule. If you're lucky enough to get a legal parking spot along the street, parking is free, otherwise it will cost you about $5 per day.

Once on the island, just about every service you'll need is within a block of the ferry dock. The tourist booth in the dock parking lot can provide you with a map of the island for $1. It will guide you to the unusual gray granite lighthouse at Sandy Point, Crescent Beach, the Clayhead Nature Trail, or the wildlife refuge at Rodman's Hollow. The map, and your sense of direction, is about all you'll need to find your way around this small island.

Across the street from the dock area you can rent a bike or moped, then shop for picnic foods at the Seaside Market next door (about the only place on the island to get provisions). While bringing your car over to the island may be cheaper than renting bikes for a family (about $10 per day per bicycle) or mopeds (about $60 per day for two), these two-wheeled vehicles bring you closer to the island's down-to-earth charm.

Most of the island's accommodations are right along Old Harbor's main street. **The National Hotel**, built in 1888, is the most prominent. You can't miss it as the ferry pulls into the harbor. Doubles are $75 to $210 depending on the season and type of view. Call (401) 466-2901 or (800) 225-2449 for reservations. **The Surf Hotel** (401-466-2241) and **The Inn at Old Harbor** (401-466-2212) with doubles including continental breakfast ranging from $85 to $140 are two other Victorian inns right in the town's center. **The Hotel Manisses** and **The 1661 Inn**, both on the edge of town, are jointly managed. Guests staying at either can enjoy a small animal farm behind the Manisses Hotel, buffet breakfasts, and dinner at the hotel. The hotel has one of the most interesting menus on the island; dinner entrées are priced from $14.50 to $26.50. Room rates range from $48 to $300 (401-466-2421).

After visiting the island you can pick up the 2 to 22 Days itinerary again by following US 1 north from Point Judith to Route 138. Take Route 138 east to Newport.

NEWPORT

Newport, on Aquidneck Island, is a city of contrasts:
from the wealthy, some of whom still inhabit turn-of-
the-century mansions, to military personnel stationed at
the naval base, to the yachting crowd that routinely
invades Newport each summer. Somehow this city
manages to satisfy all of these groups in their varied pur-
suits. Today you'll discover why.

Suggested Schedule

9:00 a.m.	Breakfast.
10:00 a.m.	Tour one of Newport's sumptuous mansions.
11:30 a.m.	Take Ocean Drive and stop for a picnic lunch at Brenton Point State Park.
1:00 p.m.	Visit another luxurious "cottage."
2:30 p.m.	Promenade along the Cliff Walk, skirting the great lawns of many of Newport's finest homes and the ocean some thirty feet below.
3:30 p.m.	See the Tennis Hall of Fame or the Touro Synagogue, or spend the rest of the after-noon browsing at the Brick Marketplace, Bannister's Wharf, or along Thames Street.
6:00 p.m.	Dinner.
8:00 p.m.	Relax to the beat of a local band in one of Newport's many bars, or watch a jai alai match.

Travel Route

All of today's driving will be within Newport itself.
Ocean Drive can be reached either from the downtown
waterfront area by following the signs to Ocean Drive or
by traveling past the mansions on Bellevue Avenue and
taking a left when you get to the end of Bellevue.

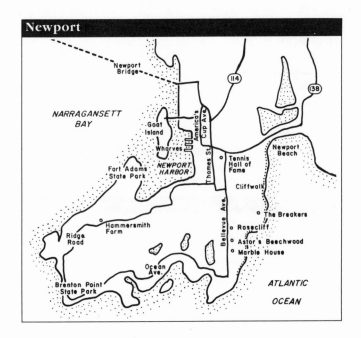

Newport "Cottages"

The Preservation Society of Newport operates six exquisite mansions, or "cottages" as they were called by their original owners, one historic home, and a topiary garden. You will probably have time to visit only two properties in one day unless you're very energetic. Take your pick:

Marble House, Chateau-Sur-Mer, and **The Elms** are open throughout the winter from 10:00 a.m. to 4:00 p.m. on weekends and are beautifully decorated for Christmas. Most of the remaining mansions are open weekends starting in April, and all are open daily throughout the summer from 10:00 a.m. to 5:00 p.m. The Breakers is open from 9:30 a.m. to 6:00 p.m. July through Labor Day. Since the hours do vary from mansion to mansion, and from season to season, it is best to check with the Preservation Society (401-847-1000) for hours during your visit. Admission to most of the mansions is $5 for adults, $3 for children 6 to 11. Reduced rates are available when you purchase combination tickets to more than one mansion. The combination tickets range from $9.50 for any two mansions to $28 if you wish to visit them all.

The Breakers, on Ochre Point Avenue off Bellevue, is the most extravagant of all the mansions and the most popular with tourists. Built in an Italian Renaissance style for Cornelius Vanderbilt in 1895, this stately home with an abundance of gold leaf and marble throughout its interior is almost overwhelmingly opulent. Children will enjoy the "Children's Cottage" on the grounds.

Chateau-Sur-Mer ("House by the Sea") and **Rosecliff** (on Bellevue Avenue) are situated on the ocean as well. Chateau-Sur-Mer has a Chinese Moon Gate on its grounds. Rosecliff was designed by well-known architect Stanford White and has the largest private ballroom in Newport. Robert Redford and Mia Farrow waltzed in this ballroom in the movie version of *The Great Gatsby*.

Marble House on Bellevue Avenue is my personal favorite. Appropriately named for the beautiful and rare marble throughout, the "cottage" was built for William K. Vanderbilt in 1892. A Chinese Tea House on the grounds exemplifies the moneyed class's fascination with the Orient at the turn of the century.

Also on Bellevue Avenue are **The Elms** and **Kingscote.** The Elms, modeled after a French chateau, is known for its array of trees and shrubbery. Kingscote, built in 1839, is one of the oldest mansions open to the public. Incorporating elements of both Victorian and Gothic architecture, the estate was named after William Henry King, who acquired the property in 1864.

The **Hunter House** at 54 Washington Street is much smaller in scale than the grand "cottages," reflecting its mid-eighteenth-century time period. It was the head-quarters for French naval forces during the Revolutionary War and is a National Historic Landmark.

The Green Animals topiary gardens are located on Cory's Lane off Route 114 north in Portsmouth. An elephant, a giraffe, and a camel are just a few of the animal-shaped shrubs that are bound to amuse children and adults alike.

Several other stately homes, not operated by the Preservation Society, are also open to the public. **Hammersmith Farms**, near Fort Adams, is often considered the most "livable" of the Newport mansions. The wed-

ding reception for John F. and Jackie Kennedy was held
here. Its colorful gardens were designed by Frederick
Law Olmsted. Open weekends in March and November,
daily April through October from 10:00 a.m. to 5:00 p.m.
At the height of the summer season, hours are extended
to 7:00 p.m.

Bellecourt Castle on Bellevue Avenue is still owned
and occupied by the Tinney family. The house is open for
high tea and guided tours by attendants in period cos-
tume. A gold coronation coach and art treasures from all
over the world are among the items on display. Admission
is $6 for adults, $5 for seniors, $3.50 for students, $2 for
children 6 to 12, and $10 for a family of two adults and
their children. The house is open daily from 9:00 a.m. to
5:00 p.m. during the summer and is closed January
through mid-February. Call (401) 846-0669 for museum
hours if you plan to visit during the spring or fall.

Beechwood, also on Bellevue Avenue, was built for
the Astors. Although the home is not as lavish or well
kept as the Preservation Society mansions, the tour can
be quite entertaining: actors playing members of the
Astor household greet you as a dinner guest and treat you
to family gossip of the day. A "calling card" is $7 for
adults, $5.50 for children and senior citizens, and $30 for
a family. The house is open from 10:00 a.m. to 4:00 p.m.
on weekends February through April, and from 10:00 a.m.
to 5:00 p.m. daily May through mid-December. It is
closed from mid-December through January.

The grand mansions of Newport are not the only
homes that merit a look while you're here. There are
many beautifully restored colonial homes in and around
Queen Anne Square one block from Thames Street.
Explore these streets on your own or take an organized
walking tour with the Newport Historical Society. The
Society is located at 82 Touro Street, and tours usually
begin at 10:00 a.m. in the summer. Call (401) 846-0813 for
additional exact schedules and cost.

Other Sightseeing Highlights

▲**Touro Synagogue**—Built in 1763, the oldest synagogue in the country is now a National Historic Site. Sum-

mer hours are 10:00 a.m. to 5:00 p.m. daily, except Saturday. Winter visitors call (401) 847-4794 for an appointment.
▲**Tennis Hall of Fame**—The museum is adjacent to the
emerald green grass courts of the Newport Casino. The
casino was built in 1880, and professional tennis tourna-
ments are still held there today. Tennis buffs will no
doubt want to visit the museum, but those who don't
play will probably be content to poke around the outside
of the building. Admission to the museum is $4 for adults,
$2 for youths under 16, or $10 per family. Senior citizen
discounts are available. The museum is open from 10:00 a.m.
to 5:00 p.m. June through September and 11:00 a.m. to
4:00 p.m. the rest of the year.

Should you wish to view the island from a two-
wheeled vehicle, you can rent bicycles from **Ten Speed
Spokes** at the corner of Elm and America's Cup Avenue
(401-847-5609).

Shopping

The Brick Marketplace on Thames Street and Bannisters
and Bowen wharves off America's Cup Avenue comprise
Newport's main shopping district. Not to be missed by
nautical buffs is the **Armchair Sailor Bookstore** on
Lee's Wharf, which has one of the most comprehensive
selections anywhere of maritime publications.

Nightlife

Jai alai is considered to be the fastest game on two feet,
and you may wish to view a match or two at **Newport
Jai Alai**, 150 Admiral Kalbfus Road. Rhode Island is one
of the few states that allows parimutuel wagering on the
sport. Admission is nominal to encourage betting, which
some find similar to playing the horses. Call (800)
451-2500 or (401) 847-4252 for schedule and information.

Many of Newport's bars and restaurants offer musical
entertainment in the evenings. Try **The Ark** on Thames
Street for jazz. **Cobblestones**, also on Thames, has live
entertainment on weekends and a piano bar. **Club
Thames** on America's Cup Avenue is the place to go for
dancing to a contemporary beat.

NEW BEDFORD AND SANDWICH

Leaving Newport's tycoons behind, you will learn about more customary nineteenth-century New England occupations such as whaling in New Bedford and glass-making in Sandwich.

Suggested Schedule

9:00 a.m.	Leave Newport for New Bedford.
10:00 a.m.	Visit Whaling Museum.
11:00 a.m.	Stroll through New Bedford's renovated historic district and sit down to an early lunch.
12:30 p.m.	Travel to Cape Cod.
1:30 p.m.	Sandwich Glass Museum.
2:30 p.m.	Heritage Plantation.
5:00 p.m.	Check into lodging.
6:00 p.m.	Early dinner and quiet evening to prepare for an early departure in the morning.

Travel Route: Newport to Sandwich (62 miles)
From Newport, take Route 114 north to Route 24 north toward Tiverton and Fall River. At Fall River get on Interstate 195 east toward Cape Cod. Take Exit 15 to Route 18 for New Bedford's historic quarter and follow signs to the visitor center.

After stopping in New Bedford, return to I-195 east. Take Exit 22A for Route 25 to Cape Cod and the Islands via the Bourne Bridge. There is a rotary at the end of the bridge. Follow the rotary three-quarters of the way around to US 6 east toward Sagamore. As you approach the Sagamore Bridge, go straight onto Route 6A east for Sagamore and Sandwich. When you get to Sandwich, there will be a sign to the center, which is about one-half mile from Route 6A to your right.

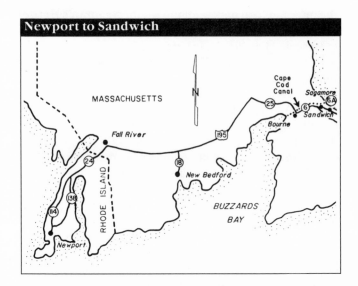

Newport to Sandwich

New Bedford Sightseeing Highlights

Once a bustling whaling center, New Bedford experienced a great decline during the twentieth century. Recently, efforts have been made to restore the city to its past glory. You can see the handsome result of those efforts by rambling through the sixteen-block cobblestone area that comprises the historic district, originally built up in the 1760s. In its heyday, 10,000 men from New Bedford made their living in the whaling trade. New Bedford's visitor center is on Second Street in the historic district. It is open Monday through Saturday 9:00 a.m. to 5:00 p.m., Sunday 11:00 a.m. to 5:00 p.m.

▲▲**Whaling Museum**—Exhibits here, ranging from model vessels and ship's logs to artwork depicting whaling expeditions, will give you a fascinating look at an industry and an era that have long since died out. Open Monday through Saturday 9:00 a.m. to 5:00 p.m., Sunday from 1:00 to 5:00 p.m. During the summer, Sunday hours are 11:00 a.m. to 5:00 p.m. Admission is $3.50 for adults, $3 for seniors, $2.50 for children 6 to 14. After visiting

the museum, you may want to visit the **Seaman's Bethel**
across the street: it was the whalemen's chapel referred to
in Herman Melville's *Moby Dick*.

▲ **Rotch-Jones-Duff House & Garden Museum**—
Built in what is now New Bedford's County Street
Historic District, this 1834 Greek Revival home is a fine
example of the "brave houses and flowery gardens"
Melville described in *Moby Dick*. The museum is open
during the summer from 11:00 a.m. to 4:00 p.m. Tuesday
through Saturday. On some summer evenings, the museum
offers concerts under the stars. Call (508)977-1401 for
more information.

Sandwich Sightseeing Highlights

The town of Sandwich celebrated its 350th birthday in
1987. It is the quintessential Cape Cod town, with well-
kept shingled houses, gentle tidal marshes, and many
sights to occupy the out-of-town visitor.

▲▲ **Heritage Plantation**—The plantation is on Grove
and Pine streets. To get there, turn left onto Grove Street
next to the town hall in Sandwich center. The parking lot
will be on your left approximately one-half mile from the
center. The prettiest time to visit the plantation is in early
June when the rhododendrons are in full bloom, but the
beautifully landscaped 76-acre grounds are handsome
in any season. American folk art, Currier & Ives lithographs,
antique firearms, and early automobiles are among the
plantation's other attractions. The antique cars, housed in
a replica of the Shaker Round Barn at Hancock, include a
vibrant green and yellow Duesenberg designed for Gary
Cooper which will delight auto buffs. The art museum
houses a carousel to entertain the children while you
view the Currier & Ives collection. Buses run at regular
intervals between the museums. Admission is $7 for
adults, $6 for seniors, $3 for children 6 to 12, and there is
no charge for children 5 and under. The plantation is
open from mid-May through mid-October from 10:00 a.m.
to 5:00 p.m. daily, although tickets are not sold after 4:15
p.m. Picnicking on the grounds is not allowed.

▲**Sandwich Glass Museum**—Across from Town Hall
Square in Sandwich center, the museum houses a fine
collection of glassware made in the 1800s by the Boston
& Sandwich Glass Company and the Cape Cod Glass
Works. Exhibits include an explanation of glass manufacturing procedures and a chronology of the Sandwich
operation. Open daily from 9:30 a.m. to 4:30 p.m. April
through October, closed during January, and open the
remaining months Wednesday through Sunday from
9:30 a.m. to 4:00 p.m. Admission is $3 for adults, $.50 for
children over 5.

In Sandwich, you can also visit a number of historic
homes all within a three-block radius of Town Hall
Square. There's a water-operated stone mill, **Dexter's
Grist Mill,** and **Hoxie House**, the oldest house on Cape
Cod, originally built in the 1600s and restored in 1960.
Admission to the mill is $1.50 for adults, $.75 for children
12 to 16. Hoxie House is open June through October
10:00 a.m. to 5:00 p.m. daily (last tour 4:15 p.m.). Admission is $1.50 for adults, $.75 for children. Combination
tickets to both sites are $2.50 for adults, $1 for children.

Yesteryears Doll Museum, in the First Parish
Meetinghouse, is open daily from 10:00 a.m. to 4:00 p.m.
May through October. Admission is $2.50 for adults, $2
for seniors, and $1.50 for children.

The **Thornton Burgess Museum,** just up the street
from the mill, was the home of the children's books
author, and some of his works and original artwork is on
display here. If you're traveling with small fans of Peter
Rabbit and the famous briar patch, then you may want to
visit **The Green Briar Nature Center and Jam
Kitchen** on Discovery Hill Road off Route 6A east of
Sandwich between Sandwich center and Quaker Meeting
House Road. You can watch homemade jams bubbling
away in the kitchen, visit "Peter Rabbit," then take the
nature trail around the "old briar patch" that served as an
inspiration for Burgess's marvelous children's tales. Both
the museum and the jam kitchen are open Monday
through Saturday 10:00 a.m. to 4:00 p.m., Sunday from

1:00 p.m. to 4:00 p.m. During July and August, there is storytelling at the museum.

Lodging
On Sandwich's Main Street, the **Dan'l Webster Inn** (508-888-3622) will bathe you in four-star comfort you won't have to sell your soul for. The dining room has a fine reputation, serving such favorites as chateaubriand ($24.95) and baked scrod in lobster sauce ($15.95). Double rooms run from $65 to $165 per night depending on the season. Reservations are strongly recommended.

Sandwich also has a handful of choice bed and breakfasts, all in the town center. **6 Water Street** (508-888-6808) next to the Thornton Burgess Museum is a spotless guest house. Breakfast, included in the room rate, is served overlooking tranquil Shawme Pond. Doubles are $50 to $95. Across the street from the Dan'l Webster, friendly hosts greet you at the **Captain Ezra Nye Guesthouse** (508-888-6142) built in 1829. Rates, $50 to $75 per night including breakfast, are quite reasonable for the area. The **Isaiah Jones Homestead** (508-888-9115 or 1-800-526-1625), also on Main Street, is elegantly furnished with four-poster beds and other Victorian pieces. Modern conveniences are not overlooked, as one room has its own jacuzzi tub. Doubles range from $65 to $110. Lovely handmade quilts adorn the beds at **The Summer House** at 158 Main Street. The inn has a pleasant sun porch, and afternoon tea and a full breakfast are included in the nightly rate of $50 to $70. Call (508) 888-4991.

You'll find a wide assortment of motor inns and cottages along scenic 6A in Sandwich. On the upper end is the mock Tudor-style **Earl of Sandwich Motor Manor** (508-888-1415 or 1-800-442-EARL), with doubles ranging from $35 to $85. The small cedar-shingled **Spring Garden Motel** (508-888-0710) with flowering window boxes is in East Sandwich on the edge of a tidal marsh. Continental breakfast is included in the room rate ($35 to $58). If you would like to wake up to a rooster crowing and other sounds of a working farm, **Wingscorton**

Farm Inn (508-888-0534), across the road from the Spring Garden Motel, offers fine accommodations ($115 to $150 per night including a full breakfast).

For those traveling on a budget, the **HyLand Youth Hostel** at 465 Falmouth Road in nearby Hyannis is not too far from the ferryboat docks. The hostel is open all year and also offers facilities for families and couples. Beds are $10 per person. Call (508) 775-2970 for information.

Camping

Shawme Crowell State Forest on Route 130 in Sandwich has 270 sites and is open seasonally (508-888-0351). **Peter's Pond Park** in Sandwich has both tent and trailer sites. Located on a freshwater pond, the campground is open seasonally June through Labor Day. Sites start at $14 per night (508-477-1775).

Dining

In New Bedford for lunch, **Freestone's Restaurant & Bar** is located in an attractive building on the corner of Williams and Second streets. It serves seafood-melt sandwiches and the like at reasonable prices; entrées are more expensive (around $12 apiece). **Jimmy Connor's Irish Pub**, on the corner of Acushnet and Union streets, is a good place to stop for a casual burger and draft beer at a modest price. **The Last Laugh** is a bar and deli just north of the historic district where you can sample sandwiches named for famous comedians such as Jackie Gleason.

For dinner, if the Dan'l Webster is too steep for your budget, try **Sandy's** (508-888-6480), a family-style restaurant just north of Sandwich on 6A. The fried clams are marvelous, but bring a hearty appetite as the portions are huge. Just a little farther north on 6A is **The Sagamore Inn** (508-888-9707), a favorite with locals. The atmosphere is very lively, and the fare includes fresh seafood, New England-style dinners, and Italian specialties. **Michael's at Sandy Neck**, on Route 6A in East Sandwich, specializes in seafood. Prices are moderate.

Nightlife
The **Cape Cod Melody Tent** in Hyannis features well-known singers, comedians, and rock groups throughout the summer. Call (508) 775-9100 for schedule and ticket information.

Itinerary Options
Bargain hunters with time to spare may profit from prospecting the New Bedford/Fall River area factory outlet stores. These stores are factory outlets in the truest sense since they are generally located on the premises of the factory. A guide to the outlets can be picked up at the New Bedford visitor center.

The world's largest exhibit of historic fighting ships can be found in Fall River's **Battleship Cove**. Visitors can tour the USS *Joseph P. Kennedy Jr.* destroyer, a 35,000-ton battleship called "Big Mamie" that saw action in WW II, a WW II attack sub, and PT boats. Call (508) 678-1100 for information. **The Marine Museum** at Fall River nearby has ship models, a Titanic exhibit, and other marine collections. The museum is open 9:00 a.m. to 4:30 p.m. Monday through Friday, 10:00 a.m. to 5:00 p.m. on weekends and holidays.

If you've got young ones who are tired of looking at historic sights, you may want to treat them to **Edaville Railroad Crafts Village and Fun Park**. Heading toward the Cape on I-195 from New Bedford, get off on Route 58 to South Carver. At Edaville, kids can take a train through cranberry bogs, a paddlewheel ship, an antique fire engine, and kiddie rides. There's also a petting zoo and a wading beach. Call (508) 866-4526 for hours and rates.

MARTHA'S VINEYARD

Although much of your New England trip so far has been spent along the coastline, where day-to-day life in the past was tied to the ocean and in some areas still is, you'll spend the next two days visiting islands whose main lifeline to "civilization" is the sea. The itinerary is planned so that you can spend one day on Martha's Vineyard and one day on Nantucket. The islands are meant to be toured at a relaxed pace, however, so you may want to travel to just one of them and spread the sightseeing highlights out over two days—or allow more time on each island if you can. The interisland ferry only runs from early July through mid-September, so if you are traveling during any other month you will probably have to limit yourself to just one island.

Suggested Schedule

8:15 a.m.	Leave Sandwich for the Hyannis docks.
9:15 a.m.	Ferry leaves for Martha's Vineyard.
11:00 a.m.	Arrive in Vineyard Haven, then travel to Gay Head.
12:30 p.m.	Have lunch and see the jagged cliffs at Gay Head.
1:30 p.m.	Leave Gay Head for Edgartown.
2:30 p.m.	Take your choice: stroll past stately mansions from the whaling era, or shop for souvenirs in lovely Edgartown, or soak up the sun on a quiet beach on Chappaquiddick or along Beach Road between Edgartown and Oak Bluffs.
6:00 p.m.	Check into accommodations.
7:00 p.m.	Dinner.

Travel Route: Sandwich to ferry docks in Hyannis (10 miles)

From Sandwich center, travel to Hyannis by Route 6A east until it intersects with Route 132. Turn right on Route 132.

When you reach Hyannis, there will be a rotary and signs to the ferry docks. (If you plan to travel to Nantucket or Martha's Vineyard for the day only, there is free parking on South Street about two blocks from the docks. The parking lots are marked by a blue shell sign with a large "P" in the center of the shell. Cars may not be left overnight in the free parking lots.) Long-term parking at the docks costs about $6 per day. Should you wish to take your car to Martha's Vineyard, you'll need to take the ferry from Woods Hole, which is described below as a route option.

Steamship Authority boats leave from South Street and travel to and from Nantucket only; Hy-Line Boats to both Nantucket and Martha's Vineyard leave from Ocean Street, which intersects with South Street. Because of their proximity to one another, and because fares from Nantucket (around $9.50 for adults and $4.75 for children) are roughly the same on both lines, it is possible to take the Hy-Line out to the islands and return by the Steamship Authority, or vice versa, giving you more departure times to choose from. Sailing time from Hyannis to Vineyard Haven is approximately one hour and 45 minutes, and roughly two hours to Nantucket (some of the Hy-Line boats can do it in an hour and 45 minutes).

You will arrive on Martha's Vineyard in Vineyard Haven. Rent a moped and ride southwest toward West Tisbury. From West Tisbury, travel along Middle Road to Chilmark, and from Chilmark follow signs to Gay Head. If you're picnicking, turn right about five miles outside of Chilmark at the sign for Lobsterville Beach. After lunch, return to the main road and continue to Gay Head to view the cliffs and lighthouse. If you didn't bring a picnic lunch, there are several fast-food establishments at Gay Head where you can get fried clam platters and the like. It is 19 miles from Vineyard Haven to Gay Head.

From Gay Head, return to West Tisbury, then follow the Edgartown-West Tisbury road to Edgartown. Total distance from Gay Head to Edgartown is 21 miles.

Martha's Vineyard

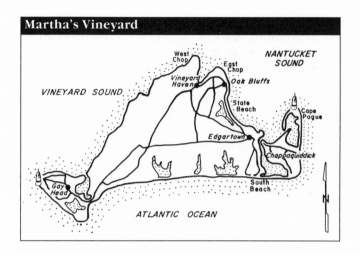

Route Option: Visiting Martha's Vineyard one day and Nantucket the next, which involves a lot of travel time on ferries and the added expense of renting alternative modes of transportation on the islands, may not allow enough time for exploration of each island. Should you decide to visit only Martha's Vineyard, take the ferry from Woods Hole instead of Hyannis. It is faster and cheaper. To get to Woods Hole from Sandwich, take Route 6A west to Sagamore, then follow US 6 west to Bourne. From Bourne, take Route 28 east to Falmouth and follow signs to the docks. The first ferry to the Vineyard usually leaves around 7:00 a.m. in the summer, and sailing time is approximately 45 minutes. Boats leaving from Woods Hole arrive in either Oak Bluffs or Vineyard Haven, only a few miles apart.

Passenger fares one-way from Woods Hole to Martha's Vineyard are around $4 for adults, $2 for children. Automobiles are $30 one-way from mid-May through mid-October and about half that during the winter months. Reservations for automobiles are *strongly* recommended during the summer months. Although it may seem expensive to bring a car over, when you consider that moped rentals are at least $50 a day, it may be worth the fare, particularly if you decide to stay more than one day or if there are more than two people in your party. Call the Steamship Authority in Woods Hole (508-540-2022) for the ferry schedule and reservation information.

Should you wish to spend all your time on Nantucket instead, call either Hy-line Cruises (508-778-2600) or the Steamship Authority (508-771-4000) in Hyannis for complete ferry information. Cars can travel on Steamship Authority ferries only, at a rate of $43 each way. Since Nantucket is such a small island, it really makes more sense to leave your car on the mainland and travel by other means once on the island.

Transportation on Martha's Vineyard
Mopeds are one of the easiest ways to get around the island. You don't have to worry about finding a parking space when you discover that deserted stretch of beach, and you can travel much faster than on a bicycle. The suggested schedule is designed for those traveling by moped; if you decide to bicycle instead, adjust your travel time accordingly. There are clearly marked and well-maintained bicycle paths on the island.

Moped and bicycle rental places abound in Vineyard Haven, Edgartown, and particularly Oak Bluffs. Many operations claim they have the lowest rates on the island. You may want to shop around, but my experience has been that rates tend to be fairly consistent from one place to the next and that your time is better spent sightseeing than looking for a bargain-priced moped rental. Daily rentals cost at least $50 in season for a moped that seats two fairly comfortably. Bicycle rentals run about $10 to $15 per day.

Numerous taxi services and sightseeing operators will greet you right at the boat and take you around the island, should you not want to get around on your own steam.

Martha's Vineyard
Though Martha's Vineyard is only 7 miles from Cape Cod and the mainland, once you get there it doesn't take long to relax and leave the rest of the world behind. The island

is 20 miles long by 10 miles wide at its widest point, and the population swells from around 12,000 year-round residents to almost 62,000 during the summer. Even so, if you venture out of the main towns, you can almost always find a quiet spot to call your own.

Martha's Vineyard was named for an early settler's daughter and for the abundance of grapes that used to cover the island. Now the island is comprised of three main towns, Vineyard Haven, Oak Bluffs, and Edgartown, with stretches of white sand beach and sand dunes in between. Edgartown, the most elegant of the three, is another example of what great prosperity the whaling trade brought to nineteenth-century New England communities. Vineyard Haven is the quietest of the three, while Oak Bluffs, with its colorful Victorian "gingerbread" houses and active nightlife, is the most flamboyant.

Most people don't come to Martha's Vineyard to spend their time in museums, but if inclement weather forces you indoors, there is the **Old Schoolhouse Museum** on Main Street in Vineyard Haven run by the Historical Preservation Society. The museum is open Monday through Friday 10:00 a.m. to 2:00 p.m. from mid-June through mid-September. Admission is by donation. Also in Vineyard Haven, the **Jirah Luce House** displays nautical and other artifacts representing nineteenth-century island life, including a collection of Victorian dolls. It is on Beach Street and is open Tuesday through Saturday 10:00 a.m. to 4:30 p.m. from mid-June through mid-September Admission is $2 for adults, $.50 for children.

In Edgartown on School Street, **The Dukes County Historical Society** operates a museum and library dedicated to preserving island history through its exhibits of maritime artifacts, scrimshaw, and antique clothing. It is open 10:00 a.m to 4:30 p.m. Tuesday through Saturday from mid-June through mid-September. Admission is $2 for adults, $.50 for children. During the rest of the year the museum is open Wednesday through Friday 1:00 p.m. to 4:00 p.m., Saturday 10:00 a.m. to 4:00 p.m., and admission is free. Other indoor island activities include shopping in Edgartown, or if you're traveling with kids, **The Flying Horses Carousel** at the bottom of Circuit Avenue in Oak Bluffs.

Back outdoors, you may enjoy an excursion to **Chappaquiddick Island**. A ferry runs from the waterfront in Edgartown to the island from 7:30 a.m. to midnight during the summer. Fares are nominal, and prices are even quoted for horses and cattle in case you brought yours along. The ferry runs as needed and must be one of the shortest ferry crossings you'll ever experience. Moped riders may not find the trip worthwhile since the main road turns to sand several miles inland, and mopeds are not meant to operate in sand. The Chappaquiddick bridge is on the far side of the island.

The beaches on the Vineyard are lovely. Perhaps the most accessible beach to the public is the **Joseph Silvia State Beach**, which runs along the road between Edgartown and Oak Bluffs. Just park your vehicle on the side of the road, hop over the dunes, and stretch out. Warning: as tempting as it may be, overnight camping is not allowed.

Helpful Hints

Those who plan to travel about the island by bicycle or moped should only bring over one small bag that will fit easily on your back or in the vehicle's basket. If you need to carry more than a daypack, be prepared to take a taxi to and from your hotel once on the island.

Lodging

For sumptuous accommodations in Edgartown, **The Charlotte Inn** on South Summer Street fits the bill while providing country inn comfort in restored nineteenth-century homes that originally belonged to sea captains. Doubles start at $195 and suites at $350 during the high season (508-627-4751). The lovely **Victorian Inn** on South Water Street was once a whaling captain's home as well and is now listed in the National Register of Historic Places. Prices are $67 to $187, and breakfast is included

(508-627-4784). **The Daggett House** at 59 North Water Street (508-627-4600) was built in 1660, has a secret stairway, and is the only B&B on the water in Edgartown. Doubles are $67 to $165 including breakfast. **The Governor Bradford Inn**, at 128 Main Street (508-627-9510), is also a handsome home originally built for a sea captain. Doubles range from $60 to $195 including breakfast.

The Oak Bluffs Inn, at the corner of Circuit Avenue and Pequot Avenue in Oak Bluffs, is painted flamboyantly in pink to exemplify the lighter side of Victorian architecture. Call (508) 693-7171 for rates and reservations. The **Wesley Hotel** on Lake Avenue overlooking Oak Bluffs Harbor has been restored and is typical of many turn-of-the-century seaside hotels. Double rooms run between $60 and $135 (508-693-6611).

The Vineyard Harbor Motel, on Beach Road leaving Vineyard Haven in the direction of Edgartown, sits on the harbor and has a nice courtyard, and rooms are equipped with refrigerators. Rates range from $45 to $110 (508-693-3334). The **Captain Dexter House** on Upper Main Street in Vineyard Haven was built in 1843 for a sea captain and now serves as a comfortable inn. Doubles range from $55 to $165 (508-693-6564), and the inn is open from May through October.

Perhaps the least expensive lodging on the island can be found at **The Manter Memorial AYH Hostel** on the Edgartown-West Tisbury Road three miles west of the airport. Dormitory-style accommodations cost about $10 per night per person. The hostel is open from April through November; call (508) 693-2665 for further information.

Camping
There are two campgrounds on Martha's Vineyard: **Webb Camping Area** on Barnes Road several miles southwest of Oak Bluffs (508-693-0233) and **Martha's Vineyard Family Campground** on the Edgartown-Vineyard Haven road a little over a mile from the ferry dock (508-693-3772). Martha's Vineyard Family Campground,

the more conveniently located of the two, is open from mid-May through mid-October; nightly rates start at $18. Webb Camping Area is open from mid-May through mid-September with nightly rates starting at $18. Both campgrounds have facilities for both RV and tent campers.

Dining

During the summer, the visitor has plenty of dining choices on the island. There are a number of family-style restaurants and coffee shops along Vineyard Haven's Main Street, but since it is a "dry town," restaurants cannot serve liquor. **Classic Capers Catering** on Beach Road in Vineyard Haven can set you up with a picnic lunch including gourmet pasta salads and sandwiches.

In Edgartown, **The Navigator Restaurant and Boathouse Bar** (508-627-4320) at the foot of Main Street and **The Wharf Restaurant** (508-627-9967) across the street both serve seafood. The Navigator overlooks the water, and lunches go for about $7.95, while dinner entrées run around $18.95. **Martha's Restaurant** (508-627-8316) on Main Street across from the town hall and **Over Martha's Cafe** upstairs are pleasant for either lunch or dinner. At lunch, Martha's Restaurant serves tasty sandwiches for about $7. Dinners lean toward pasta and seafood dishes in the $15 to $20 range. Over Martha's Cafe has a sushi and raw bar. Both are in an attractive Victorian dwelling with cheerful porch dining. If your appetite runs to entrées such as roast rack of lamb dijon, veal scaloppine, and prime rib, try the **Shiretown Inn & Restaurant** (508-627-3353). Dinner entrées start at $20, and there is a pub on the premises. **Andrea's Restaurant** (508-627-5850) on Upper Main Street features northern Italian cuisine in an elegant but comfortable setting, while **Jo Jo's** (508-627-3325) in the Colonial Inn complex on North Water Street serves more traditional Italian dishes such as manicotti and ravioli for takeout or sit-down meals at reasonable prices. For the cheapest oceanfront table in town, get a burger or fried clams to go from **The Quarterdeck** stand near the Chappaquiddick ferry, and sit on the docks.

In Oak Bluffs, meals are usually casual, and on Circuit Avenue, you can get anything from steak and seafood at **David's Island House** to subs, pasta, and pizza at **Papa's Pizza** to fresh fish at **The Oyster Bar** to Szechuan at the **Orient Express.** Or try Mexican food at **Zaboltec** (508-693-6800) on Kennbec Avenue.

Nightlife
Of the three main towns, Oak Bluffs has the most active nightlife on the Vineyard. The **Atlantic Connection Nightclub** as well as some of the neighboring bars on Circuit Avenue can be jam-packed during the summer months. Many of the patrons are college students working on the island during school break.

DAY 19
NANTUCKET

Thirty miles from the Massachusetts coast, Nantucket Island is a sparkling oasis in the Atlantic. Evidence of the island's one-time whaling prominence can be seen in the facades of graceful Federal, Greek Revival, and Georgian-style homes that border Nantucket town's cobblestone streets. Shingled cottages in Siasconset on the other side of the island are more modest, yet no less respectable, reminders of the seafaring life. In between are miles of low-lying moors and soft sand beaches.

Suggested Schedule

9:00 a.m.	Stroll around Oak Bluffs.
10:00 a.m.	Take ferry to Nantucket.
12:00 noon	Arrive in Nantucket and travel to Siasconset.
1:00 p.m.	Picnic on the beach in Siasconset.
3:00 p.m.	Return to the town of Nantucket and spend the rest of the afternoon exploring quaint narrow streets, attractive boutiques, and historic homes.
7:00 p.m.	Dinner.

Travel Route
Hy-Line (508-778-2600) operates an interisland ferry from Oak Bluffs, Martha's Vineyard, to Nantucket from June 12 to September 15. The ferry takes passengers only. The ferry departs Oak Bluffs three times a day and costs $10 for adults, $5 for children. Bikes are $4.

Once on Nantucket, travel to Siasconset by following Main Street away from the docks to Orange Street. Turn left on Orange Street and follow it until you come to a rotary. At the rotary, take Milestone Road all the way to Siasconset. Affectionately known as "Sconset," Siasconset is 7½ miles from the town of Nantucket. For bicyclists, a paved bike path parallels the main road for most of the distance.

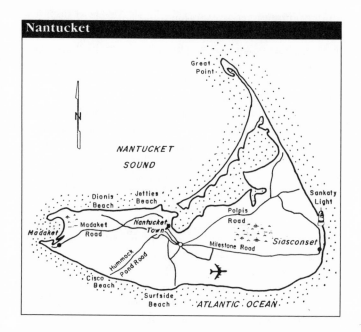

Nantucket

Sightseeing Highlights

In Siasconset, there are no official sights to see, but the town's often-deserted beach, quiet seaside lanes, and charming weathered cottages are enough to warrant the trip from Nantucket center. One of my favorite walks is along the footpath that runs between some of Sconset's most beautiful homes and the beach plum-covered sand dunes that serve as a protective barrier between the houses and the sea. To get to the footpath, go straight from the market in the town's center to the row of houses overlooking the beach. At the end of the row, at a house named "Casa Marina," turn right just to the left of the house on what looks like a driveway. Where the driveway veers back to the main road, continue straight ahead onto the lawn. This is the beginning of the footpath. The path will lead you across people's lawns—this is legal, but of course one must be considerate of their property. The path runs from the village out to Sankaty Head Lighthouse.

The Nantucket Historical Association (508-228-1894) operates a number of period homes, museums, and monuments, representing four centuries of Nantucket history. The sights are located throughout the town of Nantucket, so you should pick up the "Historic Nantucket" brochure, which maps out the route, from the tourist office on the corner of Chestnut Street, just one block from Main Street.

The tour begins at the **Thomas Macy Warehouse** on Straight Wharf, then continues to the **Whaling Museum** on Broad Street near Steamboat Wharf. Just next door is the **Research Center** housed in the Peter Fougler Museum building where genealogical charts and ship's logs are on display. The period homes include **The Oldest House,** built in 1686 and considered to be the oldest house still standing on the island; **The Hawden House,** a stately Greek Revival built in 1845 at the height of the whaling era; **The 1800 House**, decorated with Nantucket-made furniture; and **Greater Light**, converted from a barn into a summer cottage during the 1930s. You can also visit the **Old Gaol**, or old jail, built in 1805; the **Abiah Folger Franklin Memorial**, the site, on Madaket Road about ½ mile from town, where Ben Franklin's mother was born; **The Old Mill**, built in 1746 and still operational today; **The Quaker Meeting House,** dating to 1838; **The Fair Street Museum** next door, containing Nantucket decorative arts exhibits; and **The Fire Hose Cart House**, which contains nineteenth-century firefighting equipment and was built in 1866.

Admission charges to the various buildings range from $2 to $3, or you can get a visitor's pass that will admit you to all of them for $5 for adults, $2.50 for children 5 to 14. You'll need at least three hours to take the entire tour. The buildings close at 5:00 p.m., so if you wish to visit them all, you will probably have to pass on the trip to Sconset or else travel to Sconset late in the day.

The Maria Mitchell Science Center, dedicated to the nation's first prominent woman astronomer, operates a science library, a small natural science museum, an aquarium, an observatory, and the astronomer's birthplace built in 1790. The center is open from 10:00 a.m. to

4:00 p.m. Tuesday through Saturday during the summer. Stop in at the library at 2 Vestal Street, or call (508) 228-0898 for details. **The Nantucket Life-Saving Museum** on Polpis Road outside of town claims to be the only museum of its kind in the world. It is open from June 15 to October 15 from 10:00 a.m. to 5:00 p.m. Tuesday through Sunday. Admission is charged.

Those with extra time to beachcomb may also want to visit **Children's Beach, Jetties Beach,** and **South Beach,** all within walking distance from downtown Nantucket. **Dionis Beach**, three miles south of town, has still-water swimming, while more adventurous swimmers will enjoy the surf at **Madaket, Surfside,** and **Siasconset.** Serious surfers find **Cisco Beach** to their liking.

Getting Around the Island

Nantucket is small and flat enough so that you can get around rather easily by bicycle. Rentals cost about $10 per day, and you should have no trouble locating the rental shops as you come off the boat. Moped rentals are much more expensive—at least $50 per day for a two-person vehicle. However, if you can afford it, renting one may make sense since they allow you to cover much more ground in a short period of time. Most bike rental establishments also offer mopeds.

Bus service runs from Nantucket center to Siasconset and other island beaches during the summer, or you may find it more convenient to explore the island by taxi or on a guided tour. **Barrett's Tours** at 20 Federal Street operates both a taxi service and guided tours. Call (508) 228-0174 for information. **Nantucket Island Tours** on Straight Wharf also runs island tours regularly from May through October; tickets cost about $9 for adults, $4 for children (508-228-0334).

Lodging

In Sconset, your lodging choices are limited to **Wade Cottages** (508-257-6308), which has a three-night minimum, and **The Summer House Inn** (508-257-9976), which has a restaurant. Both overlook the ocean and offer pleasant accommodations. Wade Cottages opens in late May and operates through September. Room rates range from $75 to $160. Lodging at the Summer House includes private sitting rooms. Rates start at over $200 from mid-June to mid-September and are less off-peak. The inn closes for the season at the end of September.

The Jared Coffin House at 29 Broad Street in downtown Nantucket, probably the best-known inn on the island, is open all year. Guest rooms are spread out among six dwellings, the oldest dating to the 1700s. The inn also operates a respectable restaurant, with courtyard dining in the summertime, and a cozy bar. Dining prices are moderate, while doubles go for $110 to $160 (508-228-2405). **The Nesbitt Inn,** just down the block at 21 Broad Street in a large Victorian, is run by a friendly couple and is reasonably priced at $65 to $75 per night for a double (508-228-0156).

The town of Nantucket has a seemingly endless list of bed and breakfasts, yet remarkably they fill up quickly during the height of the summer. **Nantucket Accommodations** (508-228-9559) is a reservation service that can help you find a room; or you can try the **Union Street Inn** (508-228-9222) at 7 Union with accommodations ranging from $75 to $100. There is also a string of guest houses on North Water Street convenient to the town center, among them, the **Brass Lantern Inn** (508-228-4064) and **The Periwinkle Guesthouse** (508-228-9267). Room rates run from $80 to $140 at the Brass Lantern, and from $70 to $120 at the Periwinkle.

There are no campgrounds on Nantucket, but **Star of the Sea AYH Hostel** in Surfside does give budget travelers a lodging option. Dormitory-style beds rent for $10 per night. The hostel is 3½ miles from the ferry. The hostel is on the National Register of Historic Places, and its ocean-side location is appealing. Reservations are essential (508-228-0433). It is open April 1 through the end of October.

Dining

The Sconset Café (508-257-4008), in Siasconset center, serves both lunch and dinner in addition to selling its own cookbook. With entrées such as Indonesian grilled shrimp and shrimp stuffed artichokes, the café offers an interesting twist to its seafood dishes that one doesn't come across in too many New England restaurants. Lunch entrées run around $7, dinner entrées begin at $17. The café is only open during the summer, as is the market around the corner where you can pick up fresh sandwiches and pasta or potato salad to take down to the beach with you.

The Chanticleer Inn (508-257-6231), also in Siasconset, specializes in French gourmet fare and is considered by many to be the best restaurant on the island. Festive flowers and a brightly painted carousel horse greet diners in the restaurant's garden courtyard, making outdoor dining a must in good weather. The atmosphere, cuisine, and service will cost you, however, as lunch entrées start around $15, and it would be hard to sit down to dinner for less than $40 per person.

For an elaborate but pricey breakfast, try **Arno's** (508-228-5857) on Main Street in Nantucket center. Arno's has an extensive selection of omelets and breakfast entrées, such as smoked chicken benedict and smoked Norwegian salmon served with herbed eggs, that range from $5.50 to $8.75. Breakfast is served daily from 8:00 a.m. to 3:30 p.m. For a more traditional breakfast, try **The Downeyflake** on South Water Street (508-228-4533). They have terrific homemade doughnuts.

On South Water Street, **The Atlantic Cafe** (508-228-0570) and **The Rose & Crown** (508-228-2595), several doors down, both offer satisfying meals in a pub atmosphere. For casual fare, there are numerous fast-food joints on the road leading to the Steamship Authority boat dock. One of them, **Henry's Sandwiches** on Steamboat Wharf (508-228-0123), makes great subs.

Arts and Entertainment

Places like the **Rose & Crown** and **The Brotherhood** at 23 Broad offer in-town musical entertainment. **The Wind-song** (508-228-6900) at the Nantucket Inn on Macy Lane features jazz musicians, and **The Box** (508-228-9717) on Dave Street is an informal dance club. **The Actor's Theatre of Nantucket** performs popular plays, concerts, and children's matinees throughout the summer (May-October). Call (508) 228-6325 for ticket information. **The Nantucket Musical Arts Society** presents Tuesday evening concerts during July and August (508-228-3735), and **The Theatre Workshop of Nantucket** is a community theater open year-round (508-228-4305).

CAPE COD

Exposed as it is to the ocean, Nantucket tends to get beaten up occasionally by raging sea storms, yet its quiet, simple life-style seems sheltered from the outside world. In contrast, the latest trends in food, fashion, and art somehow manage to make their way out to Provincetown at the tip of Cape Cod. Once it was a stopover for the pilgrims. Today the art, gay, and tourist communities all vie for space along Provincetown's harbor, making the town a hive of activity during the summer months. Today you'll make the journey from the island of Nantucket to Provincetown, enjoying the beauty of the Cape Cod National Seashore along the way.

Suggested Schedule

8:00 a.m.	Breakfast.
9:00 a.m.	Spend your last hour and a half on Nantucket visiting a sight you missed the previous day.
10:30 a.m.	Depart for Hyannis.
12:30 p.m.	Arrive in Hyannis and begin journey to Provincetown.
1:00 p.m.	Lunch in Chatham.
2:30 p.m.	Visit the Cape Cod National Seashore.
4:30 p.m.	Travel to Provincetown and check in for the night.
5:30 p.m.	Stroll down Provincetown's colorful Commercial Street, perhaps stopping in at the Provincetown Heritage Museum or Art Association Museum.
7:00 p.m.	Dinner.

Travel Route

The suggested schedule assumes that you are traveling sometime between mid-June and mid-September. If you are traveling at any other time of year, the ferry schedule from Nantucket is much more limited, so you should call

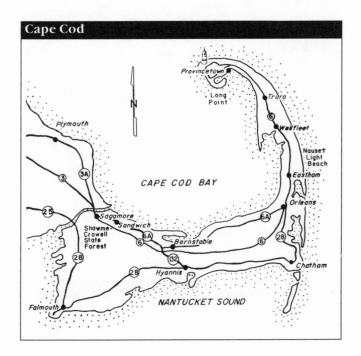

Cape Cod

either the Steamship Authority (508-228-0262) or Hy-Line Cruises (508-778-2602) for departure times during your visit.

From Hyannis, take Route 28 east to Orleans, stopping in the lovely town of Chatham for lunch. If you have time, visit the Chatham Lighthouse on Shore Road off Route 28, or drive down seaside lanes. Some of the cape's most beautiful homes are on the ocean in Chatham.

From Chatham, continue on Route 28 to Orleans where Route 28 intersects with US 6. Follow US 6 to Provincetown. The Salt Pond visitor center off US 6 in Eastham is one of the main visitor information centers for the Cape Cod National Seashore. At Truro, Route 6A will take you by oceanside motels and cottages if you're looking for simple beachfront accommodations. US 6 will take you right by the sand dunes.

Sightseeing Highlights
▲▲▲The Cape Cod National Seashore—The National Seashore stretches from the eastern half of the

cape's elbow all the way out to its fingertips at Province-town, offering the visitor miles of nature trails, beaches, and wind-sculpted sand dunes peppered with beach grass. You won't be able to cover all 27,000 acres of the seashore in one afternoon, but a ranger at the Salt Pond visitor center can send you off in the direction of Nauset Lighthouse, a good hiking trail, or a remote beach. There's a marsh trail right behind the visitor center, as well as a nature trail especially designed for the blind. You can park at Nauset Beach for $3 a day, and there is a bath-house facility available there in season. From the nearby Coast Guard Station you can see the place where Henry Beston's "Outermost House" once stood (unfortunately, it was washed away with the extreme tides brought by the blizzard of 1978). The seashore is open to the public year-round.

▲**Provincetown Art Association and Museum**— Changing exhibits include works by respected American artists such as Milton Avery, as well as promising new-comers to the art scene. The museum at 460 Commercial Street is open daily during the summer from noon to 5:00 p.m., then from 7:00 p.m. to 10:00 p.m. Admission is $2 for adults, $1 for children, students, and seniors. Call (508) 487-1750 for off-season hours.

▲**Provincetown Heritage Museum**—Artifacts per-taining to the sea make up the majority of the museum's exhibits, the focal point being the 64-foot-long half-scale model of the *Rose Dorothea*, a turn-of-the-century fish-ing vessel. It is the largest indoor boat model in the world. Admission to the museum is $2 for adults, children under 12 free. The museum is open from 10:00 a.m. to 6:00 p.m.; until 10:00 p.m. during the summer. It is on the corner of Commercial and Center streets.

▲**Pilgrim Monument and Provincetown Museum**— You will have no trouble locating the monument because, at 255 feet, it is the tallest all-granite structure in the United States. It affords marvelous views of the cape and South Shore on clear days. Museum exhibits spotlight outer Cape Cod history. Unfortunately, handicapped access is limited as there is no elevator to the top of the monument. Visitors must use ramps and stairs to climb to the top. Admission is $3 for adults, $1 for children 4 through 12. Open 9:00 a.m. to 9:00 p.m. during the summer. Call (508) 487-1310 for hours if you plan to visit off-peak.

Lodging

The Victorian **Anchor Inn** at 175 Commercial Street has a wonderful porch for people-watching, an attractive garden in front, and oceanview rooms that rent for about $105 in the summer and for as little as $55 in the off-season (508-487-0432). Rooms without ocean views are on the low end of the price range, and the inn is open throughout the year. Also open year-round is the **White Wind Inn** just across the street. Doubles go for $45 to $110. Call (508) 487-1526 for reservations. **The Somerset Guesthouse** on the corner of Commercial and Pearl streets has reasonable rates at $50 to $85 (508-487-0383). All inns listed are convenient to downtown Provincetown.

Route 6A in nearby Truro has a string of cottages and motels on the beach. Accommodations there vary in quality but are an option if you want to stay on the beach or if you are traveling with a family and find in-town bed and breakfasts too expensive for your whole crew. If you have trouble finding lodging in the area, try calling Provincetown's lodging information number, (508) 487-3424, for assistance.

Camping

Coastal Acres Camping Court on the West Vine Street Extension is the closest campground to downtown Provincetown. They do have a three-night minimum stay requirement for reservations, but you could call on the day of your arrival and see if they have space available (508-487-1700). Sites cost $17 for a tent and $23 for RV hookups. The campground is open April through October. **Dune's Edge Campground** off US 6 is just a little farther from town but still convenient and borders

on sand dunes of the National Seashore (508-487-9815).
Sites are about $18 per night, and the campground is
open May through September. In North Truro there are
three campgrounds you might try if Coastal Acres and
Dunes Edge are full. They are **Horton's Park** ($15 per
site; 508-487-1220), **North of Highland Camping
Area** ($14 per site; 508-487-1191), and **North Truro
Camping Area**, which is open all year ($7 to $14 per site;
508-487-1847).

Dining

For a different sort of dining experience, try **Old Reliable
Fish House** at 229 Commercial Street (508-487-9742). It
has a mixed menu of Portuguese and Yankee specialties.
The restaurant is on the water with outdoor seating in
season, and prices are reasonable. **Ciro & Sals** on Kiley
Court is known statewide for sumptuous northern Italian
creations. Prices are on the high end, and reservations are
strongly recommended (508-487-0049). **The Grand
Central Cafe** at 5 Masonic Place gives seafood a Mexican
treatment with dishes such as lobster enchiladas, shrimp
fajitas, and crab chile rellenos. Dinner prices range from
$12 to $16 (508-487-9116).

On the more traditional side, **Vorelli's** at 226 Commercial Street serves Italian and seafood dishes in a nice
atmosphere. Dinner entrées range from $14 to $18. The
restaurant also has a raw bar (508-487-2778). Also on
Commercial Street, **The Mew's**, which was once a stable
(508-487-1500), and **Pepe's** (508-487-0670) are popular
for seafood, while **Cafe Blase** (508-487-9465) serves
tasty sandwiches at moderate prices and has a pleasant
sidewalk cafe in the summertime. There is no shortage of
sub shops and pizza joints in town, and ice cream lovers
are bound to be tempted by Provincetown's many ice
cream parlors.

Itinerary Options

If you have more time, the Cape Cod National Seashore
has enough beautiful coastline to occupy nature enthusiasts

and beach bums alike for many a day. There is always a
new dune to investigate. Whale watching is also an agreeable pastime in this part of the world. The *Portuguese
Princess* shuttles eager marine mammal watchers daily
from Provincetown, April through November, to view the
whales in their natural habitat. Call (508) 487-2651 or
(1-800) 442-3188 for ticket information.

PLYMOUTH

In 1620, the Pilgrims actually landed in Provincetown
first before settling in Plymouth because of its protected
harbor. Today you'll follow the Pilgrims' path from
Provincetown to Plymouth and discover how they sur-
vived that first cold winter in America.

Suggested Schedule

8:30 a.m.	Leave Provincetown for Plymouth.
11:00 a.m.	Visit Plimouth Plantation.
1:00 p.m.	Lunch.
2:00 p.m.	Visit Plymouth Rock and the *Mayflower II*.
3:00 p.m.	Visit Cranberry World, Pilgrim Hall, or other sightseeing highlight of your choice.
5:00 p.m.	Check into lodging.

Travel Route: Provincetown to Plymouth (85 miles)
From Provincetown, take US 6 to Orleans. At Orleans get
on scenic Route 6A and follow it all the way to the Sagamore Bridge. Route 6A is lined with quaint Cape Cod villages, such as Barnstable and Yarmouth, where you may
want to stop along the way. Brewster has lots of antique
shops and several small museums including the **Cape
Cod Aquarium** (open daily from 10:00 a.m. to 5:00 p.m.),
the **New England Fire and History Museum** (open
Monday through Friday 10:00 a.m. to 4:00 p.m., Saturday
and Sunday from noon to 4:00 p.m.), and the **Cape Cod
Museum of Natural History** (open daily from 9:30 a.m.
to 4:30 p.m. May through mid-October, closed Monday
during the rest of the year; admission is $2.50 for adults,
$1.50 for children). From Sagamore, take Route 3 to the
Cedarville Exit (#2) and follow Route 3A north to
Plymouth. Plimouth Plantation is on your left before you
reach the town of Plymouth.

Sightseeing Highlights
▲▲**Plimouth Plantation and the *Mayflower II*—**
Both the plantation and the ship are run by the same non-profit organization. The plantation is a living museum exemplifying everyday seventeenth-century Pilgrim life and that of nineteenth-century Native Americans in the neighboring Wampanaog Settlement. In the Pilgrim village of thatched cottages, costumed guides play the parts of the original settlers tending to their farm animals, gardens, and everyday chores. They claim to know nothing of modern times but are happy to explain how and why things were done in 1627. The *Mayflower II* is docked in Plymouth Harbor adjacent to Plymouth Rock several miles away. Since historians aren't really sure what happened to the original *Mayflower*, this replica was built in England in the 1950s. On board, costumed guides relate the events of the fateful 1620 voyage, and you can see the cramped conditions under which the Pilgrims traveled. *Mayflower II* and Plimouth Plantation are open daily April through November from 9:00 a.m. to 5:00 p.m. The *Mayflower II* is open until 6:30 p.m. from late June through Labor Day. Admission to the plantation is $12 for adults, $8 for children. Admission to the ship is $5.50 for adults, $3.75 for children. Combination tickets are $15 for adults, $10 for children.

▲**Plymouth Rock**—There is nothing extraordinary about this enshrined rock other than the fact that it symbolizes the Pilgrims' first settlement and thus is a cornerstone of American colonization. Visiting Plymouth Rock is probably comparable to kissing the Blarney Stone; every true patriot should make a pilgrimage there once in a lifetime for their country's sake.

▲**Cranberry World**—Outside the museum building is a small cranberry bog where you can see how this one of only three native American fruits is grown. Inside there are exhibits on how the tangy fruit is harvested and its uses through the years. Since the museum is operated by the Ocean Spray company, there is no charge for admission, and of course samples of cranberry refreshments are also free. Cranberry World is located at 225 Water Street in Plymouth and is open daily 9:30 a.m. to 5:00 p.m., April through November. The center is open until 9:00 p.m. Monday through Friday during July and August.

▲**Plymouth National Wax Museum**—Overlooking Plymouth Rock and harbor from atop Coles Hill, the museum re-creates events in Pilgrim history using wax figures. Open daily 9:00 a.m. to 5:00 p.m., March through November. Admission is $4 for adults, $2 for children.

▲**Pilgrim Hall Museum**—The museum, which is on the National Register of Historic Places, houses actual personal belongings of the Pilgrims, including Governor Bradford's Bible and Myles Standish's sword. It is located at 75 Court Street on Route 3A in the center of Plymouth. Admission is $4 for adults, $3.50 for seniors, $1.50 for children 6 to 15. The museum is open year-round from 9:30 a.m. to 4:30 p.m. daily, except for Christmas and New Year's Day.

▲**Cordage Park Marketplace**—The marketplace, now filled with factory outlet stores and boutiques, is of interest because it stands on the site of a nineteenth-century rope manufacturing plant. The Plymouth mill was the world's largest and employed an army of workers. The prints and photographs on display throughout the marketplace will give you some sense of the factory's magnitude. Cordage Park is on Route 3A about 1½ miles north of downtown Plymouth.

▲**Pilgrim Path**—In addition to leading you to the *Mayflower II*, Plymouth Rock, and the Pilgrim Hall, this trail will lead you to other historic buildings throughout Plymouth. You'd need to spend a lot of time in Plymouth if you want to see them all, but here's a sampling of what's available:

Sparrow House, at 42 Summer Street, was built in 1640 and is the oldest house in Plymouth. Now the museum houses rotating exhibits and a craft gallery, and admission is by donation. It is open daily except Wednesday 10:00 a.m. to 5:00 p.m., late May through mid-October. The craft gallery is open through December.

The **Court House and Museum** on Town Square operated as a municipal building longer than any other court house in America. It is open daily during the summer, and admission is free. **Howland House** at 33 Sandwich Street is the only house still standing in Plymouth which an original Pilgrim actually lived in. Tours are given by costumed guides. The house is open daily from 10:00 a.m. to 5:00 p.m., late May through mid-October. Admission is $2.50 for adults, $.50 for children.

The **Spooner House,** built in 1749, was the home of Bourne Spooner, founder of the Plymouth Cordage Company. The house remained in the Spooner family until 1954, and many of the original furnishings are on display. It is open from late May through mid-October; admission is $2.50 for adults, $.50 for children.

The lovely **Antiquarian House** at 126 Water Street was frequented by Daniel Webster and has a number of unusual octagonally shaped rooms. It is also open from late May through mid-October and admission is charged. **The Mayflower Society Museum** is also housed in a beautiful home. It is the headquarters of the General Society of Mayflower Descendants, but nonmembers can visit the office and library Monday through Friday from 1:30 p.m. to 3:30 p.m.

For a map and complete listing of sites along the Pilgrim Path, contact the Plymouth Area Chamber of Commerce at 91 Samoset Street, Plymouth, MA 02360.

Lodging
The Pilgrim Sands Motel, on Route 3A, is a popular lodging choice because of its oceanfront location and proximity to Plimouth Plantation. Doubles range from $58 to $98 (508-747-0900). On a smaller scale, **The Colonial House Inn** at 207 Sandwich Street (on Route 3A south of the town center) is also convenient to sights and has reasonable rates ($50 to $80). Call (508) 746-2087 for reservations. **The Sheraton Plymouth Inn** at 180 Water Street is adjacent to the Village Landing Marketplace, not far from Plymouth Rock. Double rooms range

from $70 to $120 per night, and it is best to make reservations several weeks ahead during the summer (1-800-325-3535). **The Governor Bradford Motor Inn** is right on Plymouth's waterfront. Rooms have refrigerators and coffee makers and range from $44 to $108 (1-800-332-1620 or 508-746-6200). **The John Carver Inn** in Plymouth's town center is run by the same people who operate the fine Dan'l Webster Inn in Sandwich. Doubles range from $69 to $89. Call (508) 746-7100 or (800) 447-7778 for reservations.

Camping
Indianhead Campground, off Route 3A, south of Plymouth, is the closest camping area to Plymouth's attractions. The campground has complete hookups and recreational facilities including miniature golf, aquabikes, canoes, and rowboats. Sites start at $17 per night for two. Call (508) 888-3688 or (800) 888-3689 for reservations. **Myles Standish State Forest**, about 10 miles from Plymouth off Route 58 in South Carver, has 475 campsites plus swimming, hiking, boating, and fishing. Call (508) 866-2526 for information.

Dining
McGrath's Harbour Restaurant (508-746-9751) overlooking the harbor in downtown Plymouth is a popular spot for seafood. Lunch entrées range from $3.95 to $9.95, and dinner entrées from $8.95 to $13.95. Restaurants are plentiful all along Water Street at the waterfront. There are also informal eat-in or takeout seafood shacks out on the piers. Try **Wood's** on Town Pier where a fried clam plate for $7.95 will easily satisfy two hungry appetites.

THE SOUTH SHORE

Today brings you full circle to Boston, where your 22-day journey began. If you have time, drive through the pretty seaside villages of Duxbury, Hingham, and Cohasset, then perhaps visit the John F. Kennedy Library for an in-depth look at a president whose youth, charisma, and promise were so influential in shaping modern history.

Suggested Schedule

8:00 a.m.	Breakfast.
9:00 a.m.	Leave Plymouth for Boston traveling along Massachusetts' South Shore.
12:00 noon	Lunch in Cohasset.
1:00 p.m.	Explore Hingham and World's End Reservation.
2:00 p.m.	Visit the Adams National Historic Site in Quincy.
3:30 p.m.	Visit the JFK Library.
5:00 p.m.	Return to Boston.

Travel Route: Plymouth to Boston (40 miles)
Today's schedule assumes you are not rushing back to catch a plane. If you are, take Route 3 north to Interstate 93 north directly to Boston. The trip will take about an hour, longer in traffic.

Should you wish to return to Boston in a more leisurely fashion, take Route 3A north from Plymouth. 3A merges with Route 3 briefly, so be sure to exit for the Duxburys at 3A to continue on the coastal route. 3A will take you through the towns of Duxbury, Marshfield, Cohasset, and Hingham, but the nicest houses and best views of the ocean are off the highway. In these towns, I recommend taking back road detours to investigate the villages more thoroughly.

True to its name, Marshfield has two wildlife sanctuaries in marshy habitats: the North River Wildlife Sanctuary

The South Shore

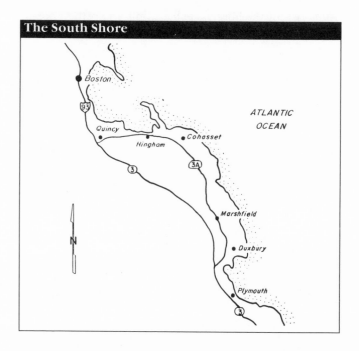

and the Daniel Webster Wildlife Sanctuary. Check with
the regional office of the **Massachusetts Audubon
Society** at 2000 Main for details on the four sanctuaries
they operate on the South Shore (617-837-9400). In Duxbury, you might want to seek out the **John Alden House**
at 105 Alden Street, home of the famous Mayflower couple, John and Priscilla Alden (open late June through
early September; admission is charged), or the **Old
Burying Ground** on Chestnut Street where Myles Standish is buried along with other passengers from the
Mayflower. In Cohasset, be sure to drive out to the harbor. In Hingham, there is the World's End Reservation,
250 acres of shoreline park designed by Frederick Law
Olmstead, whose work you've seen in the Boston Public
Gardens.

   In Quincy, follow signs to the Adams National Historic
Site. Then return to 3A, which will take you to Interstate
93 north. To get to the Kennedy Library, take Exit 14 off
I-93 to Morrissey Boulevard. Follow signs to the library.

After visiting the library, get back on I-93 north to Boston, to the airport, or to your next destination.

Sightseeing Highlights

▲**Adams National Historic Site**—The site is actually comprised of houses at several different locations which were the homes and birthplaces of U.S. presidents John Adams and John Quincy Adams, writers Henry and Brook Adams, and envoy Charles Adams. The tour of the home at 135 Adams Street is the most worthwhile of the three. Tour guides provide in-depth historical background information to go along with family artifacts. I especially enjoyed the library. If you wish to see the birthplaces as well, the tour guides can provide you with directions. The homes are open daily 9:00 a.m. to 5:00 p.m., mid-April through mid-November. Admission is charged. Children under 16 are admitted free.

▲▲**John F. Kennedy Library**—Don't let the term "library" keep you from going because you think you're going to see nothing but books. In an imposing building designed by noted architect I. M. Pei overlooking the ocean, your visit begins with a film on Kennedy. Then it's on to the exhibits, which include Kennedy's presidential desk and a time line juxtaposing Kennedy memorabilia, events in his life, and major events of the day. More than just a tribute to one man, the library gives you a fascinating look at our recent past. It also is a thought-provoking way to end the trip since it provides you with a point of reference to judge modern America against the dreams of our founding fathers whose ideals have become apparent during the past three weeks. The library is open daily from 9:00 a.m. to 5:00 p.m., closing only for Thanksgiving, Christmas, and New Year's Day. The last film of the day starts at 3:50 p.m. Admission is charged. Children under 16 are admitted free.

Dining
Kimball's by the Sea at 124 Elm Street overlooking the water in Cohasset is known for its seafood and might be a good place to stop for lunch if you're not picnicking (617-383-6050).

Boston
Boston will seem like an old friend as the city's skyline comes into view upon your return. The city is well worth getting to know better if prior obligations are not calling you home. If you must leave the area, New England's charms are certain to beckon you back for another visit.

FESTIVALS AND EVENTS

Each New England state has its share of folk festivals ranging from arts and crafts fairs to lobsterfests. These regional events are a fun way to soak up local culture, and I've listed some of the area's best and most colorful below.

Connecticut
May
Lobster Festival, Mystic Seaport Museum, Mystic
August
Railroad Days, Canaan
Governor's Cup Regatta, Connecticut River and Long Island Sound, Essex
Native American Festival, Haddam Meadows State Park, Haddam
September
Harbor Festival, New London
October
Chowder Days, Mystic Seaport Museum, Mystic
December
Festival of Light, Constitution Plaza, Hartford
Victorian Christmas, Gillette Castle State Park, Hadlyme
Christmas at Mystic Seaport, Mystic

Call (203) 566-3948, or write Travel Office, Department of Economic Development, 210 Washington Street, Hartford, CT 06106, for a complete list of Connecticut events.

Maine
January
New Year's Eve Celebration, Portland
Happy New Year's Champagne Cup, Sunday River Ski Area, Bethel
June
Old Port Festival, Old Port, Portland
July
Seafood Festival, Bar Harbor

Great Schooner Race, Rockland Harbor, Rockland
Annual Dulcimer Festival, Bar Harbor
Rockport Folk Festival, Rockport
Arcady Music Festival, Mt. Desert
August
Lobster Festival, Rockland
Maine Arts Festival, Portland
December
Christmas Prelude, Kennebunkport

Contact the Maine Publicity Bureau at 97 Winthrop
Street, Hallowell, ME 04347 (207-289-2423), for the
most current events calendar.

Massachusetts

January
First Night New Year's Eve Celebration, Boston
March
St. Patrick's Day Parade, South Boston
April
The Boston Marathon, Boston
Daffodil Festival, Nantucket
Reenactment of Paul Revere's Ride, Boston
Reenactment of the Battle of Lexington and Concord,
Lexington
May
Art Newbury Street, Boston
Salem Waterfront Festival, Salem
Wool Days, Sturbridge Village
June
Dairy Festival, Boston
Cambridge River Festival, Cambridge
Cape Cod Chowderfest, Hyannis
July
Boston Pops Concert and Fourth of July Fireworks
Display, The Esplanade, Boston
Bastille Day, Marlborough Street, Boston
Chowderfest, Boston
Tisbury Street Fair, Martha's Vineyard

Edgartown Regatta, Martha's Vineyard
Marblehead Race Week, Marblehead
Stockbridge Antique Show, Stockbridge
Yankee Homecoming Days, Newburyport
U.S.S. Constitution Turnaround, Boston
Harborfest, Boston

August

Annual Festival of Shaker Crafts and Industries, Hancock
    Shaker Village
Mayflower Lobster Festival, Plymouth

September

Eastern States Exposition, West Springfield
Bourne Scallop Festival, Buzzard's Bay
Essex Clamfest, Essex
Old Deerfield Craft Fair, Deerfield
Cranberry Festival, Harwich

October

Head of the Charles Regatta, Charles River, Cambridge
Mt. Greylock Ramble, Adams

November

Hammond Castle Museum Medieval Feast, Gloucester
Plimouth Plantation Thanksgiving Day, Plymouth

December

Christmas Stroll, Nantucket
Whale of a Christmas Celebration, Edgartown and Vine-
    yard Haven, Martha's Vineyard
Christmas at Hancock Shaker Village, Hancock

For more information on "Bay state" festivals, contact the
    Commonwealth of Massachusetts Office of Travel and
    Tourism, 100 Cambridge Street, 13th Floor, Boston, MA
    02202.

New Hampshire

May

Mountainfest, Mt. Washington Valley

June

Mt. Washington Road Race, Mt. Washington
Old Timer's Fair, Hanover
Annual Fiddler's Contest, Lincoln
Jazz Festival, Portsmouth

July
Mid-summer Arts and Crafts Fair, Loon Mountain, Lincoln
August
Mt. Washington Valley Road Rally, North Conway
September
World Mud Bowl Championships, Hog Coliseum, North Conway

Autumn Leaves Square Dance Festival, Cannon Mountain, Franconia

Railfans Day, Conway Scenic Railroad, North Conway

Miles to Isles Windsurfing Regatta, Portsmouth

Highland Games, Loon Mountain, Lincoln
October
Fall Foliage Festival, Loon Mountain, Lincoln

For more detailed information on New Hampshire festivals, contact the State of New Hampshire, Office of Vacation Travel, P.O. Box 856-RC, Concord, NH 03301 (603-271-2666).

Rhode Island
January
Polar Bears Dip, New Year's Day, Newport Beach, Newport
March
Irish Heritage Month, Newport
April
Newport Surfing Championship, Middletown
May
Newport Fun Cup Sailboarding Regatta, Fort Adams, Newport

Jaguar Festival, Newport Yachting Center, Newport
June
Secret Garden Tour, Newport

New York Yacht Club Regatta, Newport

Block Island Race Week, Block Island

International Multi-hull Festival, Newport
July
Virginia Slims Tennis Tournament, Newport Casino, Newport

Black Ships Festival, Newport

Newport Music Festival, Newport Mansions

August

New England Regional Croquet Tournament, Newport
   Casino, Newport

The International Jumping Derby, Glen Farm,
   Portsmouth

JVC Jazz Festival at Newport, Fort Adams

September

Ocean State Maritime Week, Newport

October

Aquidneck Island Harvest Fair, Middletown

November

Ocean State Marathon, Newport

December

Christmas in Newport, Newport

Call or write the Newport Tourism and Convention
   Authority, P.O. Box 782, Newport, RI 02840
   (401-849-8048), for a free descriptive brochure of
   Newport County's numerous cultural events.

Vermont

June

Hot Air Balloon Festival, Quechee

July

Summer Film Festival, Southern Vermont Art Center,
   Manchester

Volvo Tennis Tournament, Stratton Mountain

August

Vermont State Craft Fair, Killington

Bennington Battle Day Weekend, Bennington

September

Vermont State Fair, Rutland

Wurstfest, Stratton Mountain

Southern Vermont Festival of Fools, Hildene
   Meadowlands, Manchester

Stratton Arts Festival, Stratton Mountain

The Vermont Chamber of Commerce, Box 37, Mont-
   pelier, VT 05602 (802-223-3443), can provide you
   with additional information about ongoing activities
   and events in the state.

SKIING IN NEW ENGLAND

Skiing in New England is as popular with natives as leaf-peeping is with travelers. Skiing can be an invigorating way to extend your vacation and supplement the itinerary, if you're visiting the region during the winter months when many other sightseeing attractions are closed. The following list is comprised of ski areas convenient to the main *2 to 22 Days in New England* route.

Maine
Snow Bowl in Camden (207-236-3438) is a small mountain offering pleasant skiing for the whole family. **Sunday River** in Bethel (207-824-2187) is more extensive with 50 trails and a 1,854-foot vertical drop.

Massachusetts
Butternut Basin in Great Barrington (413-528-2000), **Catamount** in South Egremont (413-528-1262), **Jiminy Peak** in Hancock (413-738-5500), and **Brodie Mountain** in New Ashford (413-443-4752) are all in the Berkshire region of the state and provide skiing terrain for all levels of ability. Brodie has the greatest vertical drop at 1,250 feet, while Catamount straddles the Massachusetts and New York border. Brodie and Butternut both have cross-country trails as well.

New Hampshire
The Mt. Washington valley is heavily populated with ski areas. **Black Mountain** in Jackson (603-383-4490) and **Mt. Cranmore** in North Conway (603-356-5543) are good family mountains since they cater to all levels of ability. Mt. Cranmore's skimobile tramway is a godsend to those scared of chair lifts. **Attitash** in Bartlett (603-374-2369 or 1-800-862-1600), **Wildcat** opposite the Mt. Washington Auto Road (603-466-3326), **Cannon** in Franconia (603-823-5563), and **Loon Mountain** in Lincoln (603-745-8111) offer experienced skiers more of a challenge. Wildcat and Loon both have gondolas, and Cannon oper-

ates an aerial tramway. **Bretton Woods** near the cog railway to the top of Mt. Washington is best known for its
cross-country trails (603-278-1000). The town of Jackson
is also a major cross-country center; contact the Jackson
Ski Touring Foundation at (603) 383-9355 for information. **Tuckerman's Ravine** at Pinkham Notch is only for
the most adventurous and expert skiers. There are no lifts
so skiers must hike two and a half miles. Check with the
White Mountain National Forest Service before trying to
tackle the ravine.

Vermont

Killington (802-773-1500), with 100 trails and a 3,081-
foot vertical drop, is the largest ski area discussed here.
Nearby **Pico** (802-775-4345), outside of Rutland, is also
an enjoyable place to ski. **Bromley** in Manchester
(802-824-5522) has 35 trails, and **Stratton** (802-297-2200),
20 minutes away, is a popular ski resort as well.

As lift tickets vary from mountain to mountain, and
weather conditions vary from day to day, it is best to call
ahead for the most up-to-date information during your
visit. Dress warmly! Western skiers may be caught off-
guard by the Northeast's sometimes frigid temperatures.

INDEX

Other Books from John Muir Publications

Adventure Vacations: From Trekking in New Guinea to Swimming in Siberia, Richard Bangs (65-76-9) 256 pp. $17.95

Asia Through the Back Door, 3rd ed., Rick Steves and John Gottberg (65-48-3) 326 pp. $15.95

Being a Father: Family, Work, and Self, *Mothering* Magazine (65-69-6) 176 pp. $12.95

Buddhist America: Centers, Retreats, Practices, Don Morreale (28-94-X) 400 pp. $12.95

Bus Touring: Charter Vacations, U.S.A., Stuart Warren with Douglas Bloch (28-95-8) 168 pp. $9.95

California Public Gardens: A Visitor's Guide, Eric Sigg (65-56-4) 304 pp. $16.95

Catholic America: Self-Renewal Centers and Retreats, Patricia Christian-Meyer (65-20-3) 325 pp. $13.95

Complete Guide to Bed & Breakfasts, Inns & Guesthouses, 1991-92, Pamela Lanier (65-43-2) 520 pp. $16.95

Costa Rica: A Natural Destination, Ree Strange Sheck (65-51-3) 280 pp. $15.95

Elderhostels: The Students' Choice, Mildred Hyman (65-28-9) 224 pp. $12.95 (2nd ed. available 5/91 $15.95)

Environmental Vacations: Volunteer Projects to Save the Planet, Stephanie Ocko (65-78-5) 240 pp. $15.95

Europe 101: History & Art for the Traveler, 4th ed., Rick Steves and Gene Openshaw (65-79-3) 372 pp. $15.95

Europe Through the Back Door, 9th ed., Rick Steves (65-42-4) 432 pp. $16.95

Floating Vacations: River, Lake, and Ocean Adventures, Michael White (65-32-7) 256 pp. $17.95

Gypsying After 40: A Guide to Adventure and Self-Discovery, Bob Harris (28-71-0) 264 pp. $14.95

The Heart of Jerusalem, Arlynn Nellhaus (28-79-6) 336 pp. $12.95

Indian America: A Traveler's Companion, Eagle/Walking Turtle (65-29-7) 424 pp. $16.95 (2nd ed. available 7/91 $16.95)

Mona Winks: Self-Guided Tours of Europe's Top Museums, Rick Steves and Gene Openshaw (28-85-0) 456 pp. $14.95

Opera! The Guide to Western Europe's Great Houses, Karyl Lynn Zietz (65-81-5) 280 pp. $18.95 (Available 4/91)

Paintbrushes and Pistols: How the Taos Artists Sold the West, Sherry C. Taggett and Ted Schwarz (65-65-3) 280 pp. $17.95

The People's Guide to Mexico, 8th ed., Carl Franz (65-60-2) 608 pp. $17.95

The People's Guide to RV Camping in Mexico, Carl Franz with Steve Rogers (28-91-5) 320 pp. $13.95

Preconception: A Woman's Guide to Preparing for Pregnancy and Parenthood, Brenda E. Aikey-Keller (65-44-0) 232 pp. $14.95

Ranch Vacations: The Complete Guide to Guest and Resort, Fly-Fishing, and Cross-Country Skiing Ranches, Eugene Kilgore (65-30-0) 392 pp. $18.95 (2nd ed. available 5/91 $18.95)

Schooling at Home: Parents, Kids, and Learning, *Mothering* Magazine (65-52-1) 264 pp. $14.95

The Shopper's Guide to Art and Crafts in the Hawaiian Islands, Arnold Schuchter (65-61-0) 272 pp. $13.95

The Shopper's Guide to Mexico, Steve Rogers and Tina Rosa (28-90-7) 224 pp. $9.95

Ski Tech's Guide to Equipment, Skiwear, and Accessories, edited by Bill Tanler (65-45-9) 144 pp. $11.95

Ski Tech's Guide to Maintenance and Repair, edited by Bill Tanler (65-46-7) 160 pp. $11.95

Teens: A Fresh Look, *Mothering* Magazine (65-54-8) 240 pp. $14.95

A Traveler's Guide to Asian Culture, Kevin Chambers (65-14-9) 224 pp. $13.95

Traveler's Guide to Healing Centers and Retreats in North America, Martine Rudee and Jonathan Blease (65-15-7) 240 pp. $11.95

Understanding Europeans, Stuart Miller (65-77-7) 272 pp. $14.95
Undiscovered Islands of the Caribbean, 2nd ed., Burl Willes (65-55-6) 232 pp. $14.95
Undiscovered Islands of the Mediterranean, Linda Lancione Moyer and Burl Willes (65-53-X) 232 pp. $14.95
A Viewer's Guide to Art: A Glossary of Gods, People, and Creatures, Marvin S. Shaw and Richard Warren (65-66-1) 152 pp. $10.95

2 to 22 Days Series

These pocket-size itineraries (4½″ × 8″) are a refreshing departure from ordinary guidebooks. Each offers 22 flexible daily itineraries that can be used to get the most out of vacations of any length. Included are not only "must see" attractions but also little-known villages and hidden "jewels" as well as valuable general information.

22 Days Around the World, Roger Rapoport and Burl Willes (65-31-9) 200 pp. $9.95 (1992 ed. available 8/91 $11.95)

2 to 22 Days Around the Great Lakes, 1991 ed., Arnold Schuchter (65-62-9) 176 pp. $9.95

22 Days in Alaska, Pamela Lanier (28-68-0) 128 pp. $7.95

22 Days in the American Southwest, 2nd ed., Richard Harris (28-88-5) 176 pp. $9.95

22 Days in Asia, Roger Rapoport and Burl Willes (65-17-3) 136 pp. $7.95 (1992 ed. available 8/91 $9.95)

22 Days in Australia, 3rd ed., John Gottberg (65-40-8) 148 pp. $7.95 (1992 ed. available 8/91 $9.95)

22 Days in California, 2nd ed., Roger Rapoport (65-64-5) 176 pp. $9.95

22 Days in China, Gaylon Duke and Zenia Victor (28-72-9) 144 pp. $7.95

22 Days in Europe, 5th ed., Rick Steves (65-63-7) 192 pp. $9.95

22 Days in Florida, Richard Harris (65-27-0) 136 pp. $7.95 (1992 ed. available 8/91 $9.95)

22 Days in France, Rick Steves (65-07-6) 154 pp. $7.95 (1991 ed. available 4/91 $9.95)

22 Days in Germany, Austria & Switzerland, 3rd ed., Rick Steves (65-39-4) 136 pp. $7.95

22 Days in Great Britain, 3rd ed., Rick Steves (65-38-6) 144 pp. $7.95 (1991 ed. available 4/91 $9.95)

22 Days in Hawaii, 2nd ed., Arnold Schuchter (65-50-5) 144 pp. $7.95 (1992 ed. available 8/91 $9.95)

22 Days in India, Anurag Mathur (28-87-7) 136 pp. $7.95

22 Days in Japan, David Old (28-73-7) 136 pp. $7.95

22 Days in Mexico, 2nd ed., Steve Rogers and Tina Rosa (65-41-6) 128 pp. $7.95

22 Days in New England, Anne Wright (28-96-6) 128 pp. $7.95 (1991 ed. available 4/91 $9.95)

2 to 22 Days in New Zealand, 1991 ed., Arnold Schuchter (65-58-0) 176 pp. $9.95

22 Days in Norway, Sweden, & Denmark, Rick Steves (28-83-4) 136 pp. $7.95 (1991 ed. available 4/91 $9.95)

22 Days in the Pacific Northwest, Richard Harris (28-97-4) 136 pp. $7.95 (1991 ed. available 4/91 $9.95)

22 Days in the Rockies, Roger Rapoport (65-68-8) 176 pp. $9.95

22 Days in Spain & Portugal, 3rd ed., Rick Steves (65-06-8) 136 pp. $7.95

22 Days in Texas, Richard Harris (65-47-5) 176 pp. $9.95

22 Days in Thailand, Derk Richardson (65-57-2) 176 pp. $9.95

22 Days in the West Indies, Cyndy Morreale and Sam Morreale (28-74-5)136 pp. $7.95

"Kidding Around" Travel Guides for Young Readers

Written for kids eight years of age and older. Generously illustrated in two colors with imaginative characters and images. An adventure to read and a treasure to keep.

Kidding Around Atlanta, Anne Pedersen (65-35-1) 64 pp. $9.95
Kidding Around Boston, Helen Byers (65-36-X) 64 pp. $9.95
Kidding Around Chicago, Lauren Davis (65-70-X) 64 pp. $9.95
Kidding Around the Hawaiian Islands, Sarah Lovett (65-37-8) 64 pp. $9.95
Kidding Around London, Sarah Lovett (65-24-6) 64 pp. $9.95
Kidding Around Los Angeles, Judy Cash (65-34-3) 64 pp. $9.95

Kidding Around the National Parks of the Southwest, Sarah Lovett 108 pp. $12.95
Kidding Around New York City, Sarah Lovett (65-33-5) 64 pp. $9.95
Kidding Around Paris, Rebecca Clay (65-82-3) 64 pp. $9.95 (Available 4/91)
Kidding Around Philadelphia, Rebecca Clay (65-71-8) 64 pp. $9.95
Kidding Around San Francisco, Rosemary Zibart (65-23-8) 64 pp. $9.95
Kidding Around Santa Fe, Susan York (65-99-8) 64 pp. $9.95 (Available 5/91)
Kidding Around Seattle, Rick Steves (65-84-X) 64 pp. $9.95 (Available 4/91)
Kidding Around Washington, D.C., Anne Pedersen (65-25-4) 64 pp. $9.95

Environmental Books for Young Readers

Written for kids eight years and older. Examines the environmental issues and opportunities that today's kids will face during their lives.

The Indian Way: Learning to Communicate with Mother Earth, Gary McLain (65-73-4) 114 pp. $9.95
The Kids' Environment Book: What's Awry and Why, Anne Pedersen (55-74-2) 192 pp. $13.95
No Vacancy: The Kids' Guide to Population and the Environment, Glenna Boyd (61-000-7) 64 pp. $9.95 (Available 8/91)
Rads, Ergs, and Cheeseburgers: The Kids' Guide to Energy and the Environment, Bill Yanda (65-75-0) 108 pp. $12.95

"Extremely Weird" Series for Young Readers

Written for kids eight years of age and older. Designed to help kids appreciate the world around them. Each book includes full-color photographs with detailed and entertaining descriptions.

Extremely Weird Bats, Sarah Lovett (61-008-2) 48 pp. $9.95 paper (Available 6/91)
Extremely Weird Frogs, Sarah Lovett (61-006-6) 48 pp. $9.95 paper (Available 6/91)
Extremely Weird Spiders, Sarah Lovett (61-007-4) 48 pp. $9.95 paper (Available 6/91)

Automotive Repair Manuals

How to Keep Your VW Alive, 14th ed., (65-80-7) 440 pp. $19.95
How to Keep Your Subaru Alive (65-11-4) 480 pp. $19.95
How to Keep Your Toyota Pickup Alive (28-81-3) 392 pp. $19.95
How to Keep Your Datsun/Nissan Alive (28-65-6) 544 pp. $19.95

Other Automotive Books

The Greaseless Guide to Car Care Confidence: Take the Terror Out of Talking to Your Mechanic, Mary Jackson (65-19-X) 224 pp. $14.95

Off-Road Emergency Repair & Survival, James Ristow (65-26-2) 160 pp. $9.95

Ordering Information

If you cannot find our books in your local bookstore, you can order directly from us. Please check the "Available" date above. If you send us money for a book not yet available, we will hold your money until we can ship you the book. Your books will be sent to you via UPS (for U.S. destinations). UPS will not deliver to a P.O. Box; please give us a street address. Include $2.75 for the first item ordered and $.50 for each additional item to cover shipping and handling costs. For airmail within the U.S., enclose $4.00. All foreign orders will be shipped surface rate; please enclose $3.00 for the first item and $1.00 for each additional item. Please inquire about foreign airmail rates.

Method of Payment

Your order may be paid by check, money order, or credit card. We cannot be responsible for cash sent through the mail. All payments must be made in U.S. dollars drawn on a U.S. bank. Canadian postal money orders in U.S. dollars are acceptable. For VISA, MasterCard, or American Express orders, include your card number, expiration date, and your signature, or call (800) 888-7504. Books ordered on American Express cards can be shipped only to the billing address of the cardholder. Sorry, no C.O.D.'s. Residents of sunny New Mexico, add 5.875% tax to the total.

Address all orders and inquiries to:

John Muir Publications
P.O. Box 613
Santa Fe, NM 87504
(505) 982-4078
(800) 888-7504